Taos Adobes

Taos Adobes

Spanish Colonial and Territorial Architecture of the Taos Valley

Bainbridge Bunting

Illustrations by Jean Lee Booth and William R. Sims, Jr.

University of New Mexico Press
Albuquerque

Library of Congress Cataloging-in-Publication Data

Bunting, Bainbridge.
    Taos Adobes : Spanish Colonial and territorial architecture of the Taos Valley / Bainbridge Bunting ; illustrations by Jean Lee Booth and William R. Sims, Jr.
      p. cm.
    Originally published by Fort Burgwin Research Center and the Museum of New Mexico Press in 1964.
    Includes bibliographical references and index.
    ISBN 0-8263-1321-3
    1. Adobe houses—New Mexico—Taos Region. 2. Architecture, Spanish colonial—New Mexico—Taos Region. 3. Architecture, Modern—19th century—New Mexico—Taos Region. I. Title.
NA7235.N62T364   1992
728'.09789'53—dc20   91-39226
                                                    CIP

© 1964 by Southern Methodist University.
Originally published by Fort Burgwin Research Center, Inc.
University of New Mexico Press edition published 1992
by arrangement with Southern Methodist University.
Foreword and Bibliography © 1992 by the University of New Mexico Press.

Contents

Foreword (1992) vii

Foreword (1964) ix

The Historical-Architectural Setting 1

    The Four Architectural Periods 1

    Isolation and the Use of Native Materials 2

    Types of Surviving Houses 2

    Spanish Colonial Period 3

    Territorial Period 10

    Later American Period 13

  I. Horace Long House 15

  II. Pascúal Martínez House 23

  III. José Maria Martínez House 32

  IV. Leandro Martínez House 37

  V. José Gregorio Valdéz House 43

  VI. Sofio Fernandez House 49

  VII. The Upper Morada 54

VIII. José de Cruz House 62

  IX. Manuel Atencio House 65

  X. Policarpio Romero House 68

  XI. The Casita Martínez 74

  XII. Encarnacion Trujillo House 77

    Bibliography 80

Foreword (1992)

When *Taos Adobes: Spanish Colonial and Territorial Architecture of the Taos Valley* was originally published in 1964, it was the first detailed study of Spanish Colonial and Territorial architecture in New Mexico, and the first of several major publications on New Mexico architecture by its principal author, Dr. Bainbridge Bunting.

Unlike previous works, which focused on the "high" architecture of the region's churches and public buildings or the residences of influential citizens, *Taos Adobes* concentrates on the vernacular tradition, with particular emphasis on the distinctive architectural detailing and woodwork of these structures. As such, the work provided a solid footing for systematic study of the region's vernacular architecture and served as a sourcebook for the revival of regional detailing in the modern architecture of New Mexico.

Unfortunately, many of the structures described in *Taos Adobes* have not fared as well the book. A few, such as the Pascual Martínez House (now called the Severino Martínez Hacienda), have been restored, but others have been drastically remodeled or have fallen into ruin. Dr. Bunting later recalled with horror how publication of the book even led to the destruction of several of the sites by people searching for Spanish "treasure."

Through his courses on the history of southwestern and New Mexican architecture at the University of New Mexico, Bainbridge Bunting almost single-handedly renewed interest in the cultural geography of the region. As is evident from *Taos Adobes*, he encouraged and directed his students in the detailed recording and study of historic structures, spearheading the first sustained Historic American Buildings Survey (HABS) effort in the state since the 1930s. A tireless researcher, he contributed a series of fine articles as co-editor of *New Mexico Architecture* magazine and published several noteworthy books: *Of Earth and Timbers Made* (1974), *Early Architecture of New Mexico* (1976), and *John Gaw Meem: Southwestern Architect* (1983). Dr. Bunting left a legacy in his students, many of whom have gone on to study and publish works on the cultural geography and vernacular architecture of the region.

While subsequent studies have expanded our knowledge of the vernacular architecture of the region, *Taos Adobes* remains a classic source from which we can continue to learn.

Boyd C. Pratt

Foreword (1964)

This volume is one of a series of publications on the history and ecology of New Mexico and adjacent areas published by the Fort Burgwin Research Center, Inc., a non-profit foundation created by the late Ralph M. Rounds for scientific and educational purposes. *Taos Adobes* is the result of studies conducted at the request of the Research Center during the summers of 1960 and 1961 by Dr. Bainbridge Bunting, Associate Professor of Art at the University of New Mexico. The purpose of this still continuing project was to record, through photographic coverage and detailed architectural drawings, several of the delightfully picturesque old adobe buildings in the Taos area. Although these houses are a unique heritage of New Mexico, many of them were in advanced stages of decay and ruin. Indeed, several of the buildings described in this book have recently been destroyed.

The field research for the project was performed under Dr. Bunting's supervision by Lee Booth Sims and William R. Sims, both students of the University of New Mexico. All of the drawings and sketches reproduced in this volume are by Mr. and Mrs. Sims, except those of the Valdez House, which were done by George Bales, David Bliss, and Reginald Richey, also students at the University of New Mexico. The photographs not otherwise credited are by Dr. Bunting.

Several individuals were particularly helpful during the project. Mr. John Gaw Meem, distinguished architect in Santa Fe, and Mr. George Pearl, an outstanding architect in Albuquerque, gave valuable assistance and advice. Mr. Leandro Martinez, Santa Fe, Mr. Jacob Bernal, Ranchos de Taos, and Mrs. Amelia Chacon, Penasco, all generously put in many hours of their time and gave us the benefit of their unique personal knowledge of local history. On behalf of the authors and the Research Center, we wish to express our thanks for this assistance.

Fred Wendorf
Southern Methodist University

The Historical-Architectural Setting

An awareness of the continuity which links the past and the present is too often absent in American culture. Despite numerous dramatic reminders of the earth's geological evolution, such as the Grand Canyon and the Mississippi Delta, evidences of architectural growth and change are relatively rare. Compared to many other areas of the world, it appears that man's architectural history, in most parts of the United States, began only the day before yesterday.

A conspicuous exception, however, is New Mexico, where man has been building permanent buildings for something like 1,000 years and where structures as much as 700 years old are still standing. The area around Taos is particularly rich in old buildings—buildings which reflect an inter-mingling of architectural forms from different cultures and a piling up of layers of construction from successive epochs—much as one finds in such places as Mexico or Italy.

THE FOUR ARCHITECTURAL PERIODS

Within the 700-year span, four distinct periods are apparent in New Mexico: Indian, Spanish Colonial, Territorial, and Later American. Very broadly speaking, most of the Indian building in the Taos area dates after 1200; the Spanish Colonial Period embraces the eighteenth and early nineteenth centuries; the Territorial, the post-Civil War period; and Later American, the twentieth century.

Indian architecture in the Taos area can be categorized into the Pueblo IV and V Periods. The Pueblo IV Period, embracing roughly the years 1275-1598, followed the Great, or Classical, period of Pueblo Indian culture, during which Mesa Verde and Pueblo Bonito at Chaco Canyon were built. During the Pueblo IV period, the Pueblo Indians migrated into the Rio Grande Valley and built their multi-storied housing complexes, of which Taos Pueblo is the best surviving example. The Pueblo V Period began with the arrival of the Spanish settlers in 1598 and continues to the present. Important architectural additions to Taos Pueblo were made during both periods.

Permanent Spanish settlers came to New Mexico in 1598, and in 1610 Santa Fe was selected as the administrative center of the area. Unfortunately, almost no remains of Spanish residential construction survive from this early period because of destruction during the Indian Revolt of 1680-1692. From this pre-Revolution period, only the walls of a few churches and wall fragments of a handful of houses survive. Essentially, then, remains of Spanish Colonial residential architecture in New Mexico postdate 1692, the year De Vargas recaptured Santa Fe.

Mexican independence from Spain in the nineteenth century had no specific architectural effect on New Mexico except, perhaps, to exaggerate the isolation and self-sufficiency of the remote northern province. Buildings of the Mexican era, therefore, merely continue the Spanish Colonial tradition.

The Territorial Period, from a political standpoint, embraces the period between 1848, the year in which New Mexico was annexed to the United States as a territory, and 1912, the year of statehood. Architecturally, however, the Territorial style did not come into vogue until after the Civil War, when the Territory began to attract large numbers of merchants, miners, and ranchers, who brought the new architectural forms with them from the States. In centers like Las Vegas and Santa Fe the Territorial fashion was on the wane by 1900, but it persisted in some remote villages of the region until the building of modern highways, in the 1930's.

TAOS ADOBE

The Later American era in architecture began at different times in different parts of the state. Ordinarily it followed closely in the wake of modern transportation. The Santa Fe Railroad reached Las Vegas in 1879 and Albuquerque in 1880, but some mountain villages remained quite isolated until the Second World War. The degree to which a community's architecture reflected the Territorial style or the varied currents of Later American architecture is directly proportional to the degree of its isolation.

ISOLATION AND THE USE OF NATIVE MATERIALS

In the Taos region, until comparatively recent years, poor transportation facilities and underdeveloped technology have always limited man in his building to the materials immediately at hand—the earth itself and the trees that grew from it. Restricted to these materials, the range of his architectural forms was limited. Despite major differences in the way various social groups located and organized their dwellings—the Indians of Taos in five-story communal houses, the Spanish in clusters of one-story houses, and the "Anglos" (those persons not of Spanish or Indian parentage) scattered out over the countryside—the basic unit of composition was always the cube-shaped room of mud walls and flat mud roof.

Only in recent decades—when new materials such as concrete block, cement plaster, glass, steel casements, and asphalt or corrugated iron roofing were introduced into the area—has a fundamental change in architecture occurred. In comparison with recent changes the variations wrought in adobe and wood by earlier generations of Indian, Spanish, and "Anglo" builders seem minor indeed.

Adobe, a word of Arab origin, means "earth from which unburnt bricks are made." Technically speaking, it is a balanced mixture of clay and sand —enough sand to keep the dried clay from cracking and enough clay to give the dried mixture strength. But this adobe, which Taoseños have used so well for centuries, is highly transient. When water runs over it or moisture dampens it at ground level, it softens and sloughs off. Unless plastered and repaired, adobe walls erode away. In any uncared for adobe structure, erosion at the ground line undermines the wall on the outside until it topples outward.

Adobe roof construction is equally transient. The thick layer of earth heaped on rafters over a covering mat of saplings or boards causes rapid decay. Unless protected by some kind of watertight covering, the wood framework will rot out and need to be replaced in 75-100 years. Although an adobe building neglected for 25 years will deteriorate to the point where it is not worth repairing, given constant care it may last for seven centuries, as is true of Taos Pueblo.

So, in the use of native materials lies a historical paradox. Despite the strong historical continuity of the region's architecture as a whole, most individual buildings are distressingly short lived. Because adobe also lends itself well to remodeling, old structures can be so easily and drastically changed that little trace of their earlier appearance remains. Thus, once technology changes, a method of building that had existed for centuries disappears within a generation.

This is what is happening in New Mexico today. For this reason, the series of photographs and measured drawings which the staff of the Fort Burgwin Research Center has been systematically compiling in the last few years will be of value as a historic record and of unique interest to those who cherish the old traditions.

TYPES OF SURVIVING HOUSES

Aside from certain houses in the Indian pueblos, the "old" houses in New Mexico of today are of four kinds. There are those which "look" old. Yet a house built only twenty years ago, but since neglected, may now appear to be quite ancient; indeed, Hollywood producers have devised a system of "antiquing" brand new adobe structures within a matter of minutes by simply playing water hoses over them. A mere weather-beaten appearance, then, is no certain criterion of antiquity. Secondly, some structures of recent date have purposely been designed to appear old; these are sometimes charming, but they tell us nothing about history.

A third category comprises those structures of nondescript, though modernized, appearance which incorporate foundations, walls, and even whole rooms of early date, but which have been recently remodeled to make them more comfortable. Structures of this kind, unfortunately, reveal far less of their original character than if they had been built of stone or even of wood. This visual transciency is the principal reason why a study of early residential architecture is so much more difficult in New Mexico than in Europe or along the Atlantic Seaboard. Numerically the largest, this third group is the source of only limited architectural-historical information.

The fourth category of old New Mexican houses —particularly fruitful in the preparation of this study—consists of structures built only 80-100 years ago and not too drastically remodeled. Because technology and the economy even at this late date did not differ too radically from that of former centuries, houses built this late probably resemble earlier ones to a great extent.

SPANISH COLONIAL PERIOD

Effect of Defense Needs

All through the Colonial and Mexican periods, settlers were grouped closely in villages. Relatively few families lived on haciendas in the country for fear of Indians. During the second half of the eighteenth century the situation was particularly bad. At one point in 1760 Comanche depredations in Taos Valley were so severe that most Spanish inhabitants abandoned their own homes to seek protection within the walls of Taos Pueblo. In the 1770's Indians again harassed the area on several occasions. With the exception of the 1680 Rebellion, this danger came not from the Pueblos but from nomadic Plains Indians and Navajos who came to the settled areas on plundering expeditions.

During this difficult era the Spanish settlers huddled together in small fortified communities called *plazas*. The idea of the plaza-centered town was, of course, well known to the Spanish, but their towns in Mexico from early Colonial times had not been fortified. In New Mexico, however, the term *plaza* connoted the idea of a fortified place rather than a central square. By constructing contiguous houses about a central open area, windowless outside walls could serve as a defense barrier. The center of the community could be approached only by means of a wide, double gate. In case of attack, livestock could be corraled in the open plaza, the gates barred, and the enclosure defended.

Taos, Ranchos de Taos, Trampas and Dixon were early Spanish communities of this kind. Ranchos de Taos, originally called *Las Trampas de Taos*, had numbered 36 families of 160 persons in 1765, but the inhabitants deserted the village for the protection of Taos Pueblo during the 1770 Indian raids. In 1779, however, the community was surrounded by a defense wall and could defy a new Comanche attack.

Trampas was a similar fortified *plaza*, because in 1760, when Bishop Tamarón granted the inhabitants permission to build the present church, he stipulated that it must be situated inside the walled compound. As for Taos itself, the present location is different from the eighteenth century site which was on lower ground and nearer the river.

Even the present multi-storied "apartment houses" of Taos Pueblo were fortified in 1776. Fray Dominguez describes two building complexes on opposite sides of the river connected by walls which contained defense towers and entrance gates. Within the protected area was a special group of houses built for the Spanish settlers who were seeking asylum there.

Another protective device, in addition to the walled compound, was the defense tower called a *torreón*. One such tower stands on the property of the José Vigíl family, which acquired its land early in the eighteenth century. In 1776 the family was one of the few in the Taos region living away from the safety of the fortified Taos Pueblo compound. According to the present owner, the original *torreón* until about 1910 had a second story of logs, which connected with the adobe-walled ground floor by means of a trap door and a ladder. In case of attack, the men defended the tower from the six-sided log ramparts above, the women and children staying in the circular room of adobe below. Of another large *torreón*, which stood until the 1930's in Los Cordobas, only a few foundation stones are today in place.

The village of Dixon, originally called Embudo, in the Embudo Valley, still has two *torreones*. Standing about 150 feet apart, they seem to have guarded the corners of a compound and to have been connected by the line of outside walls of contiguous houses. One of these towers, today serving as a pig sty, is still roofed; the other is reduced to crumbling foundations. The houses of the southern half of the Dixon compound appear to have been demolished to make room for modern stores along the present highway. According to Fray Dominguez, the eighteenth-century inspector of Franciscan missions in New Mexico, fourteen families lived in Embudo in 1776, when the population was 69 persons.

Besides the walled villages, a few haciendas, large enough to see to their own defense, existed in isolation in the country. In 1740, for example, there were four such ranches in the Taos Valley. Windowless, having no outside doors except the main gate and turning inward onto a *placita* or patio, these establishments were in effect private *plazas*. Although modified later the Pascuál Martínez house in Ranchitos well illustrates this building type, even to the roof-top "shooting gallery," where defenders could guard the house from behind adobe ramparts (Chapter II).

Attached to the house on the rear was a second courtyard, surrounded by barns and store rooms and used as a corral. In the late eighteenth century, when the land near Taos was divided among a few big ranch owners, these large, patio-centered houses were probably more common than they are today.

THE END OF THE INDIAN THREAT

About the time of the Civil War, the U.S. government turned its attention to the control of nomadic Indian groups. Troops were distributed throughout the Territory and forts were constructed. The early military establishments in New Mexico consisted of small garrisons housed in temporary log stockades, or cantonments. Cantonment Burgwin was established near Taos in 1853. A replica of the original fort, based on contemporary sketches and on excavations, was built in the 1950's on the original site to house the Fort Burgwin Research Center.

The first group of buildings at Fort Union, begun in the summer of 1851 and also constructed of logs, was built by the 77 soldiers then stationed at the fort. Later, however, the garrisons were enlarged and the forts made more commodious. This phase of fort building is illustrated by the quarters of the third Fort Union, erected after 1863, which were constructed of adobe and were much more comfortable than the early log shelters.

Once the Indians were under control, villages could disperse as farmers built homes nearer their fields. Communities like Llano Quemado, Talpa, and Peñasco illustrate this stage of the development. Here houses dispersed in clusters and sometimes organized as family compounds, were built on higher land overlooking the fields in the valleys. The bottom land, watered by *acéquias* (irrigation ditches), was too precious agriculturally to be built upon. That these new houses were no longer conceived in terms of defense is indicated by the Leandro Martínez house of 1862 (Chapter IV), especially when it is compared to the Pascuál Martínez house of some forty years earlier situated next door (Chapter II). The front veranda and large outside windows indicate that Don Leandro apparently felt little threat from the Indians.

HOUSE PLAN AND ROOM USE

Certainly any description of Spanish Colonial residential architecture in New Mexico must be in large part hypothetical. Because unmodified houses from the eighteenth or early nineteenth centuries no longer survive, one must piece together a picture of what they might have looked like from bits of information gathered from excavations, from surviving fragments, and from later structures.

However, given the very conservative nature of New Mexican culture between 1700 and 1846, it seems justifiable to assume that the Pascuál Martínez house (Chapter II), as it was built in 1824, probably did not differ too drastically from a hacienda constructed a century earlier. Because the region's economy and technology changed comparatively so slightly during the Colonial Period, little incentive or capacity existed to modify architectural expression.

No single type of Spanish Colonial house plan dominates in Northern New Mexico or is typical of the period. Many persons think of the patio-centered plan as characteristic of Spanish residential architecture, but most houses in New Mexico were not large enough for so ambitious a plan.

THE HISTORICAL-ARCHITECTURAL SETTING

Only a few dwellings in the Taos area, represented by the Horace Long and the Pascuál Martínez houses, were big enough to extend about a *placita* (Figures 4 and 24). Much more common are houses of a single-axis or L-shaped plan, like the José de Cruz and the Manuel Atencio houses in Trampas (Figures 77 and 84).

Beginning modestly with two or three rooms, such houses could easily be added on to, sometimes seven or eight rooms resulting. Passage through such houses is like going through a series of connected railway coaches. Often the single-axis house was built against the hillside, all windows and doors being on the downhill side.

The widths of rooms in Spanish Colonial residences in New Mexico do not vary greatly because the roof span is limited by the load a moderately large log can carry—from thirteen to fifteen feet. For this reason, the only way a room can be made larger is by increasing its length. *Salas* are sometimes as much as forty feet in length.

The smaller the house, obviously the less possibility there was of specialized room use. Often the kitchen served as living room as well as bedroom. In larger dwellings, however, certain rooms were often set aside for special uses. A *sala*, of somewhat greater length than the other rooms, was used for more formal occasions. Unusually pretentious homes, such as the Durán hacienda at Talpa, even had a private oratory or chapel. Sometimes, several related families might live in a large compound, sharing its central patio, as well as the corrals and barns situated in the rear of the residential quarters.

WINDOWS

To people today, the most striking characteristic of the original Spanish Colonial dwellings in New Mexico would be the scarcity of windows. Because almost no window glass was available for many years, perhaps none at all until it was freighted over the Santa Fe Trail in the 1850's, windows were small, often barred with vertical poles and closed with wooden shutters.

Sometimes, on the other hand, Spanish builders, like the Indians, placed sheets of translucent mica over the window openings. No example of this limited fenestration survives today in a Spanish house, although a mica sheet about fifteen inches square with rounded corners is still in place in a house at Acoma Pueblo. Until the 1856 Pentitente *morada* of Arroyo Hondo was remodeled in 1962 (Chapter VII) its minimal fenestration was probably like that of an early house. Viewed from the outside, it appeared as compact as a piece of sculpture.

As for barred windows, the usual iron *rejas* (grilles) of both Mexican and Spanish architecture were absent in New Mexico because of the scarcity of iron. When even a simple iron barred window is discovered, as in the José Maria Martínez house in Ranchitos (Chapter III), it is probably a later addition.

In recent times, since larger and greater numbers of windows have been introduced, the visual effect of geometric solidity of Spanish Colonial architecture has diminished. For this reason, most modern Colonial style houses having sufficient and large enough windows for modern living do not look "authentic." In today's house, interior space, expressed on the outside by large windows, has become more important than the protecting shell of thick adobe walls.

DOORS

Like windows, the doors in old houses were smaller and less common than they are today. They were often lower than six feet, and the sill was sometimes raised. A plausible explanation for this low door, aside from the smaller stature of the people of that period, is that a person passing through a low opening is required to bend over, a position unfavorable to self-defense if one is forcing an entry.

In simple houses, in which little hand-shaped lumber was used, the openings between rooms often had no door at all, only a cloth curtain. Sometimes these openings were arched slightly, but no examples of true arches have been observed in the Taos area. Indeed, the only known example of true arch construction in Colonial New Mexico is in the ruined church of the Pecos Mission, built no later than 1625 and abandoned in 1838.

Because of the scarcity of metal for hinges in the colony until the days of the Santa Fe traders, builders often resorted to a primitive pintle hinging device. In the door of the chapel of the Arroyo Hondo *morada* (Chapter VII), the wooden stile on one side is extended beyond the top and bottom rails. The extensions are cut to a peg shape and fitted into sockets of the threshold and lintel to allow the door to rotate. This type of door is known in New Mexico as a *zambullo* door.

ADOBE WALL CONSTRUCTION

The walls of almost all permanent Spanish Colonial structures were built of sun baked adobe brick. Introduced to Spain by the Moors, this construction technique was brought by the Spaniards to New Mexico. Previously, the Indians had used adobe, but they did not know the technique of making brick. They laid their mud walls in solid courses or layers, about two feet in thickness. Shaped by hand, each layer had to dry before the next was added.

Good examples of this type of "puddled," or "coursed," adobe construction can be seen in a few ancient rooms at Picuris Pueblo and at the Pot Creek ruins, dating roughly about 1150 and excavated between 1959 and 1962 by Dr. Fred Wendorf, Director of the Division of Anthropology, Museum of New Mexico, and Director of the Fort Burgwin Research Center. The Indians also sometimes used chunks of adobe, rather turtle-like in appearance and set in mud mortar, but they did not employ regular brick shapes until after the Spanish came.

Another notable difference between Spanish and Indian construction is that the Indians did not set their adobe walls on stone foundations; they laid their first courses of adobe directly on the ground. Spanish builders, on the other hand, formed a rough stone foundation on the leveled ground. These foundations were too crude and shallow to equalize all settling, but they at least prevented some erosion at ground level.

Spanish-built walls are characteristically thick; in a one-story house, they are customarily between eighteen inches and two feet; in churches, they may be as much as seven feet in thickness. Indian walls, on the contrary, are often dangerously thin. It is a matter of luck or the providence of ancient gods that some multi-storied stone walled structures in certain Hopi villages, for example, have stood so long.

Batter, an inward inclination of the outside surface of walls, seems to be common in all adobe construction—from ancient Egypt to present-day New Mexico. Structurally, it is quite proper for masonry walls to get thinner as they go higher and have less weight to carry. Also, the tops of adobe walls are gradually eroded by wind and rain, which accounts for the soft, rounded silhouettes of adobe construction. Finally, the wall is frequently made deliberately thicker at the base to compensate for the expected erosion at ground level.

OTHER CONSTRUCTION MATERIALS

Besides adobe, several other materials were used for construction purposes in early periods of New Mexican history. Near the mountains, where timber was more readily available, logs were sometimes employed. The logs were frequently cut flush with the end walls, and the surfaces were often plastered over with mud to resemble regular adobe masonry. In barns and store rooms, however, the log ends were usually left projecting, as seen in structures still in use in Trampas and Talpa.

Sometimes the logs, positioned in vertical stockade style, were embedded in the ground, such as the original structures of Fort Burgwin, located in the Pot Creek Valley in the midst of the big timber. In places other than Taos, a primitive Indian type of construction called *jacál* was sometimes employed by the Spanish, as well as the Indians. Small timbers were supported in a vertical position either by horizontal grooved rails at the top and bottom of the wall or else they were woven together by willow branches. The surface was mudded over. Good examples of the Spanish use of *jacál* can be found in settlements on the east slope of the Manzano Mountains.

In certain sections of the Southwest other than Taos, builders had available a neatly coursed stone which broke naturally into square-edged, horizontal blocks. From early Indian times, masons in these sections built walls of stone set in adobe mortar. Examples of this handsome type of masonry can be seen at Spanish villages in the upper Pecos Valley, such as Villanueva, or the seventeenth-century missions on the east slopes of the Manzano Mountains. Long before the coming of the Spanish, however, magnificent stone masonry had been laid by the Pueblo Indians at Pueblo Bonito, circa 1050-1200.

ROOFS

The Spanish constructed roofs essentially like the Indians, by spanning the interior space with *vigas* (horizontal beams) and covering these with smaller pieces of wood loaded with enough adobe earth to keep out rain water and to provide insulation. By grading the adobe fill as well as controlling the pitch of the *vigas*, water was directed toward specific points of discharge, where an opening in the parapet and a *canale* (water spout) threw the rain free of the adobe walls. Care was taken to avoid draining water onto the roof of adjacent buildings, and wherever possible drainage was away from the prevailing southwesterly winds, which might drive the drainage against the wall and cause erosion. When *canales* are not kept in good repair, drainage from the roof quickly causes serious erosion of adobe walls.

CEILINGS

Several methods were employed to span the interval between the *vigas*. In pre-Spanish times the Indians, as can still be seen at Mesa Verde or Aztec Ruins, laid small saplings across the *vigas*. Called *latias* by the Spanish when they used this technique, the saplings were arranged in herring-bone patterns or set at right angles to the *vigas*. They were often painted different colors by both the Spanish and the Indians.

The Spanish sometimes split the saplings into *latias labradas* and placed them with the flat side down. Two other modifications of *latia* construction are *cedros* and *savinos*. These terms designate the type of wood employed: *cedros* are crudely split cedar poles, and *savinos* are *latias* made of unsplit juniper. The Spanish word *savín* translates as red cedar or juniper.

Still another means of covering and spanning between *vigas* is the use of adzed boards, called *tablas* or sometimes *tablones*. These differ from the later sawn board coverings in that the individual *tabla* is short, extending ordinarily only from one *viga* to the next. These short boards slant up and down, depending on the irregularity of the top of the *viga*.

The confusing terminology for these secondary ceiling members comes about because of the use of different terms in various sections of the state. One old builder in Taos referred to *latias* as *rajas* and as *varallitas*. In the southern part of New Mexico, the meaning of the terms *tablas* and *savinos* is sometimes switched. George Kubler, in his authoritative book on the Colonial churches of New Mexico, defines the term *savinos* as "cedar twigs." He also uses the term *sebogeta* instead of *tabla* for rough-hewn roof planking.

Whatever the method of covering and spanning between *vigas,* the covering members were laid over with a layer of bark, chamisa, or straw and then packed with six to twelve inches of earth to form the roof. The purpose of the bark covering was to minimize the fall-out into the room of the final earth roof covering.

Later, when "Anglo" traders offered cotton muslin at reasonable prices, this material was sometimes tacked on the ceiling under the *vigas*. Stretched tight, this *manta de techo* was painted with a mixture of flour and water; the flour gave it a white color to resemble plaster and the water shrank the cloth tight.

The advantages of this *manta* were several: the cloth provided another barrier to the dirt that silted out of the roof packing, it hid the "old-fashioned" and uneven *vigas*, and it simulated the plaster ceilings used in "proper" houses in the States. Nailing strips along the walls, as well as torn fragments of fabric, are still visible in many old houses, including the José Maria Martínez house in Ranchitos (Chapter III) and the Romero house in Peñasco (Chapter X).

In Spanish times the *vigas* were usually peeled of bark but left round. In an important room they might be adzed to a rectangular shape. But it was only after the "Anglo" sawmills began to provide sawn lumber that squared members were commonly used. Often these were decorated with a hand-planed bead molding along the edge. The first saw mill in Taos was built at Six Mile Creek, Moreno Valley, by Wilfred Barton Witt, who came from Arkansas. According to Witt's great grandson,

TAOS ADOBE

Jack Boyer of the Kit Carson Museum in Taos, operations began sometime between 1855 and 1860 and continued until the 1880's. The location of the sawing operations was changed several times when adjacent timber reserves were exhausted. According to Mr. Boyer, squared vigas with beaded corners were a specialty of the Witt Mill.

FLOORS

After 1860, sawn boards for floors and roofs became as common as squared beams and posts for houses. According to the descendants of Leandro Martínez, his house (Chapter IV) built in Ranchitos in 1862, was the first in the Taos area to have a wooden floor. In all earlier houses, Indian and Spanish alike, floors were of packed earth. Animal blood mixed with ashes was sometimes added to make the earth hard and resistant to water. Susan Magoffin makes frequent mention in her book of the earth floors in the Rio Grande Valley, the need for frequent sprinkling with water to keep down the dust, and the use of local woven carpeting known as (*jerga*) in more important rooms.

Wooden floors, first introduced in New Mexico in the 1840's, were long a mark of prestige. James Webb, describing New Mexico as he remembered it in 1844, commented that the wooden floor in the Sena store on the Plaza in Santa Fe was the "only plank floor in New Mexico except a store in Taos built by Mr. Branch and . . . perhaps Turley's Mill has one or two rooms floored with plank." Older earth floors under more recent wooden ones still exist in several early New Mexican churches. In some rooms of the *morada* of Arroyo Hondo (Chapter VII), packed earth floors are still used.

ORNAMENTATION

The Spanish Colonial house in New Mexico was built without elaborate ornamentation—in strong contrast to the fine paneling, the carved mantels, and the elaborately turned balustrades of houses built by the English colonists on the Atlantic Seaboard. If any ornaments were used at all, such as on a *portál* or a principal door, they were of sturdy wooden construction. Save for one church altar in Santa Fe, no carved stone work was apparently done in New Mexico.

In a typical *portál*, the cross beam which carried the roof *vigas* was supported by large, round vertical posts of wood. Between the post and the beam a carved bracket, called also a corbel bracket or, by the Spanish, a *zapata*, was frequently interposed. The ends of these brackets often had an intricate profile, but the sides were usually plain.

The José Gregorio Valdéz house in the Lomita district of Taos features a splendid Spanish Colonial *portál* (Figure 53). Not only is the entire 21-foot length spanned by a single beam, but the *zapatas* are an integral part of the beam itself, resulting in a high degree of decorative interest but a complete disregard for structural efficiency. The beam with its four *zapatas* are carved out of a fourteen-inch timber, which is cut back to an eight-inch depth between the *zapatas*. Thus, the effective depth of the beam is reduced from fourteen to eight inches at precisely the points where, in terms of engineering efficiency, the member should be thickest.

The decoration of the outer face of the *zapata*, characterized by a design of chisel gouges, is somewhat unusual. A purely utilitarian *portál*, on the other hand, can be seen in the José Maria Martínez house, where no corbel is used and where the vertical post and horizontal beam are mortised (Figure 36).

Corbels of elaborate profile are sometimes found in churches, in important rooms of houses, and in entrance *zaguanes*. The churches at Trampas and Ranchos de Taos are equipped with some of the finest corbels in New Mexico. Simpler corbels are still to be seen in one room of the Pascuál Martínez house (Chapter II), and in the *zaguán* of the Narcisio Rivera house, just down the river from it.

INTERIORS

The interiors of Spanish Colonial houses are ordinarily lacking in special architectural features. The walls are plastered with the same earth used for the bricks. Yet nature provides an astonishing variety of soft colors that make for extremely beautiful interior "plaster." Not every soil, however, is appropriate for plastering. Usually each community has a clay pit where a usable mud is obtained for plaster, a fact which accounts for the uniform color of the local houses. The earth selected is carefully screened and applied with the bare hands. When the plastered area has dried, it is smoothed over once more with a piece of dampened sheepskin.

A dado of darker colored adobe plaster was often used around the lower part of the wall, and a built-in adobe bench occasionally ran along one side of the room. In the nineteenth century, lengths of brightly printed muslin, brought over the Santa Fe Trail, were sometimes tacked along the lower part of the walls to keep the whitewash from rubbing off on the occupants' clothes.

Because the original wall openings in most adobe houses were few, the dominant wall surfaces of the individual room interior represented a clear geometric form. But because adobe walls are seldom straight, either vertically or horizontally, or the corners square, the wall surfaces often have a gentle undulation or bulge. This undulation softens the rooms' geometric shape. Indeed, the very austerity of the rooms accounts for their spatial clarity and beauty.

FIREPLACES

Fireplaces were used in most rooms, though sometimes they were later replaced by more efficient "Yankee" cast-iron stoves. In New Mexico, fireplaces were traditionally located in the corner and were quarter-round. They were raised on a low hearth, their face inclined slightly inward, and the opening of the fire chamber was elliptically shaped. Above the mantel shelf, a narrow flue was cased out from the corner by thin adobe bricks. That such flimsy, unlined chimney flues were far from fireproof is evidenced by many charred *vigas* and roof sheathings. However, because the walls and roof were mainly of mud, flue fires did not easily spread. Many corner fireplaces, which do not seem to be differentiated by any special name from the general term *fogón*, are still in use in Taos.

That these corner fireplaces follow an old form is indicated by those in the late eighteenth-century Spanish community house of *Casita Vieja* at El Rito, Rio Arriba County, which Dr. Herbert Dick excavated in 1958. Occupied at least as early as 1801 and probably much earlier, the Casita contained both conventional corner fireplaces and a special kind of fireplace built in the angle between the main wall surface and a low spur wall thrown out at right angles from it to form a corner. This arrangement was unintelligible to the excavators until they saw this type of fireplace standing in the Horace Long house near Ranchos de Taos (Figure 15). The low spur wall, called in dialect the *paredcito*, served as a wind break and facilitated the arching over of the fireplace opening.

In addition to these two types of relatively small corner fireplaces, a larger one featuring a bell-shaped hood over the firebox was once fairly common. By reason of its shape, this type was called a *fogón de campana*. Only two specimens survive in Taos. One of these is the unique fireplace, having two openings, in the José Gregorio Valdéz house (Figure 51), and copied recently on a smaller scale in the restoration of the Kit Carson Museum. The other, featuring an enormous flue, is in the former meeting room of the Arroyo Hondo *morada* (Figure 74).

Still one other fireplace design of considerable interest is situated in the Sofio Fernandez house in Llano Quemado (Chapter VI). It features a long, stout wooden beam which extends the full length of the room and projects into the end walls. This beam supports at one end a smoke hood built of thin, two-and-one-half inch thick adobe brick; at the other end, a shelf of hewn planks.

Because the shelf is long enough to serve as a bed, this construction is sometimes called a "shepherd's bed fireplace" and is said to have been used in shelters of sheep herders. Old residents of Taos, however, identify it as the usual cooking fireplace of earlier times, and they do not associate it with a shepherd's bed. Besides the example at Llano Quemado, the only other known surviving example is in the old Frank Applegate house in Santa Fe, today the L. J. Wolgamood residence.

Two additional points about New Mexican fireplaces are of interest. One concerns the conventional fireplace placed against a flat wall and provided with a projecting chimney-breast. This type, which often contains a wood casing of some kind, is clearly of "Anglo" derivation.

The second point concerns the Indians' use of

fireplaces. Although they had developed in very early times flue-like ventilator shafts for their underground kivas, they did not know the true fireplace prior to Spanish contact. In his extraordinarily interesting study on the architecture of Zuñi, Victor Mindeleff illustrates and describes a *piki* hearth having three ceremonial fire boxes united under a single hood.

This beam-supported fireplace hood bears a resemblance to the Spanish "shepherd's bed fireplace." That this type of fireplace pre-dates Spanish occupation is not generally argued, and the drawing that Mindeleff made in 1886 might well illustrate an old yet post-Spanish construction. Fireplaces with a flue built into the wall were not used in Europe until about 1200.

CUPBOARDS

A number of cupboards having hinged or pintle doors set into the walls of houses must once have been used in the Taos region. Although no such cupboards were discovered in the houses discussed herein, fine examples of them were acquired in the Taos area during the 1920's by collectors like Mabel Dodge Luhan and Frank Applegate. These cupboards were equipped with doors that were sometimes paneled and sometimes filled with punched tin work or fitted with spindles.

The cupboard under the window in Room #1 of the José María Martínez house (Figure 38) is characteristic of later Territorial work. The planed lumber and delicate moldings of the window and cupboard indicate that this feature is much later (circa 1860's) than the 1833 date of the house itself.

The Romero house in Peñasco has a secret compartment under an inconspicuous shelf in Room #10 which is disguised by a false wall of adobe (Figure 100). Access to the compartment is gained by pulling out the bottom shelf board. This is the only tangible evidence found by the author thus far of a secret hiding place. Yet "hidden treasure" constantly lures some people, who believe that every large house contains a concealed hoard. In recent times, treasure hunters have despoiled more old houses in New Mexico than has the erosion of wind and rain.

TERRITORIAL PERIOD

The first wave of American architectural influence on the Southwest was the so-called Territorial style. A belated step-daughter of the American Greek Revival, this style did not flourish in New Mexico until after the Civil War. The Territorial style was slow in getting to New Mexico. Although American traders began to travel the Santa Fe Trail as early as 1823 and United States military forces occupied the area in 1846, few evidences of eastern architectural influences existed prior to the Civil War's end. Because accurately dated buildings are rare, the precise chronology of the Territorial movement in New Mexico is yet to be established. However, most of the area's Territorial structures likely date after 1865. For example, the remodeling of the Palace of the Governors in Santa Fe, which added Territorial *portál* and window trim, was designed in 1861, but its execution was delayed until the autumn of 1865.

When one recalls that the Greek Revival began in cities along the Atlantic Seaboard as early as 1820, a time lag of some forty years is indicated for New Mexico. The westward progress of the style was gradual. In the forties it penetrated the Ohio Valley and Western Reserve; in the fifties it reached the Mississippi and prior to the Civil War moved up the Missouri River to outposts like Independence, Missouri, and Shawnee Mission, Kansas. But the long migration of the style across the plains was deferred until the War's termination. When this occurred, it reached New Mexico as soon as any intermediate towns in Kansas, such as Junction City or Hutchinson.

The theory that the Territorial style came into the Rio Grande Valley from northern Mexico is untenable. Leading cities in central Mexico never adopted the Neo-Classical movement, which was so popular in Europe and of which the Greek Revival is an off-shoot, because of the War of Independence, beginning in 1810. Following liberation from Spain, Mexico was too plagued by civil war and economic dislocation to do much serious building. Furthermore, a survey of cities in northern Mexico such as Chihuahua and Durango, through which the style would have had to spread to reach New Mexico, reveals no traces of nineteenth century Greek Revival forms.

The Greek Revival manner, once rooted in the

THE HISTORICAL-ARCHITECTURAL SETTING

Territory, proved exceptionally tenacious. In centers like Santa Fe and Las Vegas, the style reigned unchallenged through the 1880's, and it continued to exert a major influence on domestic design until almost 1900, when it was finally edged out of fashion by a variety of styles brought into New Mexico from the Midwest or from California.

In out-of-the-way mountain communities, however, Territorial forms were being repeated until the Great Depression. Charming folk variations on the old Greek Revival pedimented lintel and paneled door were being constructed in the villages above Peñasco by a carpenter and furniture maker named Alejandrino Gallegos, who lived until 1935. Such work in remote villages is clearly a matter of architectural survival rather than an indication of the flurry of new "Period" revivals which appeared in cosmopolitan centers in the 1920's.

The old Spanish Colonial traditions in architecture did not begin to give way until the impact of "Anglo" economy and government was felt in the post-Civil War era. The great influx of American settlers and the development of commerce after 1865 had a decided effect upon the architecture of New Mexico.

Processing and manufacturing facilities, such as saw mills and brick plants, were set up in the Territory for the first time, and improvements in the transportation system made available a wide variety of manufactured products and tools. This was in sharp contrast to the earlier period, when New Mexico, isolated and forgotten, had been forced to be almost entirely self-sufficient.

SAWMILLS AND SMOOTH-SAWN LUMBER

Shortly after Yankee occupation, sawmills were brought into the Territory from the "States" and set up in several localities. Prior to that, the shaping of a wooden beam had been a major undertaking. Either it was adzed by hand or, at best, it was sawn with a long saw manned by two workers, one standing above the log and the other pulling the saw from a pit below.

Even as late as 1879, in Santa Fe, workmen building Sister Blandina's Trade School had to shape the timbers by hand because there was no sawmill in the immediate locality. Some areas had sawmills earlier, however. A crude mill was in operation near Glorieta Pass by the middle fifties, and Wilfred Witt built his sawmill near Taos sometime before 1860. Planing mills and factories to produce doors, sash and wood trim followed the establishment of sawmills. What was probably the first planing mill in New Mexico was established in Las Vegas in 1879.

The availability of inexpensive, smooth-sawn lumber made profound changes in the architecture of Taos and of New Mexico. Although most buildings retained the traditional, thick-walled adobe core, wooden trim became more elaborate and played a role of increased visual importance. Houses sprouted front verandas, pitched wooden roofs, cased and shuttered windows, bay windows, and picket fences.

Inside wooden floors were added, as were also paneled door and window reveals, splayed window jambs and wooden fireplace casings. Such elaborations, of course, required improved metal tools and inexpensive nails as well as the supply of lumber. These items now became available as the result of easier transportation. Wagon trains along the Santa Fe Trail in the 50's and 60's carried an ever-increasing volume of merchandise and during the late 70's the western terminus of the railroad edged constantly nearer to New Mexico.

WINDOW GLASS

After sawn lumber, it was imported window glass which most affected New Mexico's architecture of the Territorial Period. New houses were provided with an increased number of windows, and in old dwellings new windows were cut through the adobe walls or the early small windows were enlarged.

Because of the reduced Indian threat, at least in the Taos area after 1853, windows were even placed in outside walls of patio-centered houses. These new windows generally followed the then-current "Anglo" preference for double-hung sash. At first home-made, the sash and trim could, after 1879, be brought in by train from Chicago or bought at the new planing mill in Las Vegas. Such luxuries as bay windows were usually reserved for residences in the larger centers, such as Las Vegas or Santa Fe.

TAOS ADOBE

OTHER MATERIALS

Improved transportation facilities also provided New Mexico builders with new roofing materials and with iron stoves. At first the wagon trains brought sheets of terneplate, a thin sheet iron plated with an alloy of lead and tin. Manufactured in sheets one foot wide and two feet long and crimped together in a seam that stood out from the surface of the roof, these sheets could be much more easily handled by the wagon trains than the much larger sheets of corrugated iron which only appeared with the advent of the railroad.

Just as metal roofs were more water resistant than the old adobe roofs, so cast iron stoves were more efficient than fireplaces and soon began to replace them. Indeed, some dwellings built in railroad towns after 1880 had no fireplaces at all but only brick flues for coal-burning stoves. Taos, however, more remote from the railroad and therefore less accessible to importations from the States, continued to employ old-fashioned fireplaces and flat mud-roofed rooms longer than railroad communities.

BRICK AND LIME KILNS

One other technological advance that affected building came with the "Yankees." This was the building of brick and lime kilns. Despite the importance of tile and brick to the architecture of Spain and Mexico, kiln-burned brick was not produced in New Mexico until well into the Territorial Period. The first bricks used in the buildings at Fort Union had to be transported from St. Louis. And even as late as 1879 Sister Blandina had to sponsor the construction of brick and lime kilns in order to obtain the materials with which to build her Girls' Trade School in Santa Fe. Because Taos never established a brick kiln of its own, structural or decorative forms of brick are relatively rare there.

NEW HOUSE PLANS

A new type of house plan appeared in New Mexico with the Territorial style. Two or three rooms deep, in contrast to the string of single rooms in the Spanish Colonial dwelling, this plan also featured a central hall that ran the full depth of the building. This hall was sometimes wide enough to serve as the *sala*, or drawing room. The symmetry of this plan reflects the more formal room arrangement of the Greek Revival in the eastern United States. The Leandro Martínez house of 1862, built just north of the older Pascuál Martínez residence, is a splendid example of the new plan (Figure 45).

By and large, fewer Territorial style buildings are found today in the Taos Valley than in the adjacent valleys of Embudo or Mora. This is undoubtedly true because of the subsequent remodeling of so many Taos buildings. Since 1945 numerous Spanish owners have "modernized" old family homes by adding cement plaster and steel casements.

On the other hand, during the 1920's and 1930's many new "Anglo" owners sought to restore the building they were acquiring to the older and then fashionable Spanish Colonial style. Remodeled and extended by 1923, the Harwood house, today the Harwood Foundation in Taos, illustrates this restoration movement.

ORNAMENTATION

The most easily recognized characteristic of the Territorial style is the triangular-shaped lintel (Figure 90). Featuring either a plain facia or one augmented by combinations of moldings, this pedimented lintel was for many years a badge of modernity in New Mexico. And, although this wood embellishment is sometimes quite intricate and charming, it is essentially superficial decoration—something added to the basic adobe core of the structure, whose structural function had not changed from Spanish Colonial times.

Such Territorial decoration, constructed of wood, is concentrated mainly at window and door openings. The other focal point for fancy Territorial ornament is the *portál*. In this period the veranda posts were more often mill-sawn than round, and to their squared faces a variety of wooden moldings, were nailed at top and bottom. These moldings, which replaced the profiled *zapatas* of Spanish Colonial times, slightly resemble the capitals and bases of Classical columns. Houses of Spanish

THE HISTORICAL-ARCHITECTURAL SETTING

Colonial plan often have representative Territorial trim, but this probably is the result of remodeling.

One other Territorial feature which one finds in some parts of New Mexico is a coping of kiln-burned brick to cap the adobe wall. Constructed of courses of brick which alternately project or are inset, such copings bear a remote resemblance to Classical cornices. But this brick wall topping is not an inevitable characteristic of the style, and in areas where pitched roofs are common or where brick was difficult to obtain, the coping is often omitted. Such copings are, therefore, comparatively rare in Taos.

The detailing of Territorial buildings in some parts of the state, such as in Las Vegas, is often astonishingly close to standard Greek Revival prototypes in the Midwest, but the style in New Mexico is most charming when least "correct." To the more austere Greek Revival formula, Territorial craftsmen sometimes added a touch of intricate jigsaw work derived from the somewhat later Queen Anne style. This style was an English reaction of the 1860's against the artificial and formal qualities of nineteenth-century academic architecture. It attempted to return to the informality and sound craftsmanship which were thought to be still present in England as late as the reign of Queen Anne—hence the name.

The style spread to the American Seaboard by the mid-70's, and its picturesqueness and informality made it particularly popular for American suburban homes until the 1890's. In the United States, however, regard for sound craftsmanship too often deteriorated into massive arrays of lathe and jigsaw work, while the original search for relief from Renaissance symmetry and formality evolved frequently into an orgy of picturesque effects that were more visual than functional.

Remote from the centers of American architectural fashion, New Mexico often mixed up the sequence of the imported styles. To compound the confusion, Colonial houses were often "up-dated" with "modern" Territorial ornament when available window glass made remodeling desirable. Hence, more hybrid than "text-book-pure" examples prevail in Territorial architecture. Excellent examples of the addition of Territorial trim to older Spanish Colonial houses are the patio doors of both the Horace Long and the Pascuál Martínez houses. The Leandro Martínez veranda, on the other hand, fuses Greek Revival motifs and Queen Anne scroll work (Figure 43).

The more remote the area, the less "correct" its "Greek" expression was likely to be. In the upper reaches of the Embudo Valley some particularly inventive if ungrammatical variations of the Greek Revival motifs are to be found. The ingenious paneled doors and the hand-planed wooden trim used in this area often have a vitality and inventiveness that the more academically correct work lacks. A splendid example of "Rio Grande Greek" is the double door composition of the surviving *portál* of the Romero house in Peñasco which, with its intricately fitted moldings, constitutes an excellent example of folk art (Figures 90 and 91).

INTERIOR FURNISHINGS

Yankee visitors and traders who recorded their impressions in diaries or travel accounts present interesting data on interior furnishings. Susan Magoffin, as a recent bride from Kentucky, accompanied her husband to New Mexico in 1846 on a merchandising trip. In describing the *sala* of the Gaspár Ortíz house, she says: "Her house, I suppose, is one of the best in the city. The entrance is into a large courtyard—the fashion of all houses—with portals all around. The long salon to the front is the sitting room. This is furnished with cushions, no chairs, two steamboat sofas, tables, a bed, and other little fixtures." Most New Mexico interiors, however, were even more sparsely furnished. Mattresses covered with blankets were placed around the walls. Chairs and bedsteads were rare and the commonest article of furniture was the chest.

W. H. Davis, a merchant from the East Coast in the 1850's, stated: "At the present day, although there are American mechanics, but few of the people have adopted our style of furniture, but cling to that of olden times. Every article of this description sells at a price enormously high and ordinary pine furniture costs more than that made of mahogany in the Atlantic States."

LATER AMERICAN PERIOD

From 1880 on, New Mexican architecture began to reflect still other "Anglo" architectural enthusiasms, but taste in the Territory always lingered well behind the tide of fashion in the "States." Prominent in New Mexico among these later fashions were: the Italian Villa, Huning Castle, Albuquerque, 1882; the French mansard-roofed Clegg mansion, Springer, 1880; and the astonishing Queen Anne Polhemus house of 1890 in Santa Fe. Around 1900 the architectural contest was waged between proponents of the Richardson Romanesque and a new wave of Classicism inspired by the Chicago World's Fair of 1893. But these movements were more often confined to bustling transportation and commerical centers and they left Taos undisturbed in her dreams of Territorial and Colonial grandeur.

Of greater importance to the architecture of New Mexico, and to Taos in particular, were the years encompassing the First World War. While the rest of the nation experimented with a series of Period Revivals—half-timbered Medieval, gambrel-roofed Dutch Colonial, mansard-roofed French, tile-roofed Spanish, and the like—New Mexico began to discover her own, unique architectural past. Sometimes termed the "Santa Fe Style," this regional offshoot of the Period Revivals sought to combine Pueblo Indian and the Spanish Colonial traditions.

The first indication of this local movement was the 1904 remodeling of Hodgin Hall on the University of New Mexico Campus; another early work of importance is the 1913 Art Museum in Santa Fe. However, unquestionably the most distinguished work in this vein was done by John Gaw Meem in the 1930's and 40's in structures like the Laboratory of Anthropology and El Cristo Rey Church in Santa Fe or his early buildings for the University of New Mexico in Albuquerque.

In Taos, two excellent representatives of this movement are the Harwood Foundation of about 1923 and the charming series of houses built by Mabel Dodge Luhan between 1923 and 1939. An even more exotic example of this romantic Period Revivalism in Taos is the extraordinary pink Muscovite residence built in the late twenties by the painter Leon Gaspard.

I. Horace Long House
Ranchos de Taos, New Mexico

Old and slowly crumbling, the Horace Long house, a patio-centered structure, is situated a mile west of Ranchos de Taos between Cordillera Road and the north bank of the Rio Chiquito. Uninhabited for the past five years, it is now used as a stable. Because of the characteristic Spanish-American division of estates among heirs, the land on which the house stands has now been partitioned through the middle of the patio, and each owner manages his portion of the property as though it were unrelated to the other.

In the summer of 1961, portions of the west side of the complex were partially demolished for the building material they still contained. The east half of the building is somewhat better preserved, but it is overgrown with weeds. Overlooked by neighbors and tourists alike, the mansion nevertheless possesses one of the finest surviving Spanish Colonial entryways and doors in northern New Mexico.

Horace George Long, one of its earliest owners and builder of at least part of it, was one of the first Yankee settlers in Taos. Born in Kentucky in 1803, he crossed the plains in the thirties and settled in Taos in 1839. Later he migrated once again and pioneered the settlement of Trinidad, Colorado, where he was living as early as 1861 and where he was a leading citizen.

While living in the Taos Valley, he was a distiller and tavern keeper, both of which operations he carried on at home. The still was situated just below the *acéquia*, or irrigation ditch, which separated it from the dwelling and supplied the necessary cold water for still operations. The tavern seems to have been located in Room 2 (Figure 7).

A tree-ring analysis of two logs used in the roof of Room 7 in the west wing of the house reveals that they were cut in 1810 and 1816. Unfortunately, it was not possible to obtain the owner's consent to take log samples from the east and best preserved section of the building. The cutting date of a log is, of course, no proof of a building's date of construction. The wills of early New Mexico inhabitants sometimes bequeathed certain *vigas* (beams) in a house along with other valuables to the various heirs. And, in some instances, *vigas* from an early building are known to have been reused in a later one.

Because no written data has come to light concerning the Long house, the reconstruction of its history must be hypothetical. However, because of the tendency of New Mexico houses to be enlarged over the years and because of the slightly larger scale and finer detailing of the rooms of the east section, it may be argued that the west rooms, numbered 7, 8, and 9, were built first (Figure 3). They might easily date from soon after 1816, as suggested by tree-ring analysis, while the rest of the building might have been added by Horace Long after his arrival in 1839.

Four architectural elements are noteworthy in this dwelling: the *placita* (patio), the ramp, the tavern room, and the *zaguán*. The *placita* was once surrounded on all four sides by rooms that allowed only one point of entry, the main gate (Figures 1 and 2). Some of these surrounding rooms long ago collapsed, but piles of earth from the disintegrated walls and roof covering still indicate their location. To the southwest, for example, the elevated level of earth clearly traces the position of rooms that closed that corner of the patio.

In the northeast corner, only the outside wall remains, to a height of some four feet, serving now as a garden wall. The impending demolition of the remaining three rooms on the west will eliminate all feeling of the once enclosed *placita,* and the remaining structure to the east will then resemble the more common single-axis houses of the area.

The living quarters grouped about the *placita* were a single room in depth, undistinguished by size or decoration. Unlike other such houses, it did not have a large *sala,* or reception room, unless this feature was situated in one of the corner areas which have disappeared. Situated on the north side of the *placita* is the well, protected by a small gabled and latticed well-house—still commonly used in most rural Taos dwellings.

Quite without parallel in existing New Mexico buildings is the ramp that leads from patio level to the roof top (Figure 5). Its substructure is solid adobe, and old residents say that this ramp once consisted of adobe steps that led to a second-story smoke house. Built of logs, the walls of the smoke house once had a series of narrow slits just under the roof to emit smoke. However, all traces of the smoke house have vanished.

The big room (Room 2) just underneath the location of the former smoke house contains a curious 16-foot intermediate wall which juts into the room on the west side and whose likely function was support for the smoke house (Figure 7). Furthermore, the ceiling supports here are doubled and set at right angles like a raft (Figure 8).

The third noteworthy feature of the house is also associated with Room 2. This room does not connect either with the *placita* or with the other interior rooms, an exceptional arrangement for patio houses. The explanation may be that the room served as Horace Long's tavern. The intermediate wall at the west end probably not only supported the smoke house but seems to have had an inside window that may have been used in dispensing food and drinks. On the north wall, below a window that looks onto the *zaguán,* is an ingenious cooling shelf (Figure 9). Against the center of this north wall is also a characteristic New Mexican "corner" fireplace with its protruding *padercito,* or baffle (Figure 15).

Finally, the Long house's most important architectural aspect is the *zaguán,* or entranceway, that leads from the main gate to the *placita* (Figures 1 and 2). Wide enough for farm wagons to pass through and entered by means of a double gate, the *zaguán* is roofed over like the rest of the rooms on the east side of the patio. Its stout wooden doors were barred on the inside and constructed to withstand the onslaughts of Indian or brigand. They are equipped with splendid hand-forged iron hardware, especially the triton-shaped hinges and rough iron studs (Figures 2 and 15).

True to Mexican and Spanish tradition, one of the big double doors includes a smaller pedestrian gate, which could be barricaded with wooden bars. This gate, featuring hand-hewn jambs, a mortise and tenon lintel, and excellent hand-wrought iron fittings, is the finest surviving example in the Taos area and perhaps in all of New Mexico.

Figure 1. Main facade. All openings except the zaguán gate and left door to the cantina were later additions. Photograph HABS, Jack Boucher.

Figure 2. Zaguán door is wide enough to accommodate a wagon; smaller inset door is for pedestrians. Photograph HABS, Jack Boucher.

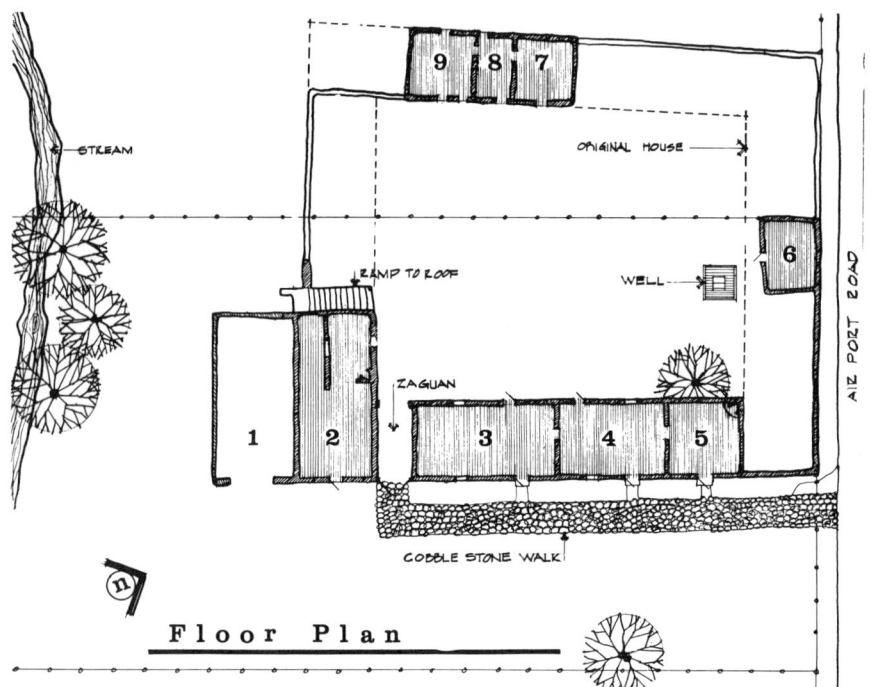

Figure 3. Location of original walls, indicated on the plan, can be traced on the ground by piles of earth.

Figure 4. View of placita showing the zaguán and the ramp to the roof; in the foreground are remains of perimeter wall.

Figure 5. Ramp of solid adobe that led to a smokehouse on the roof.

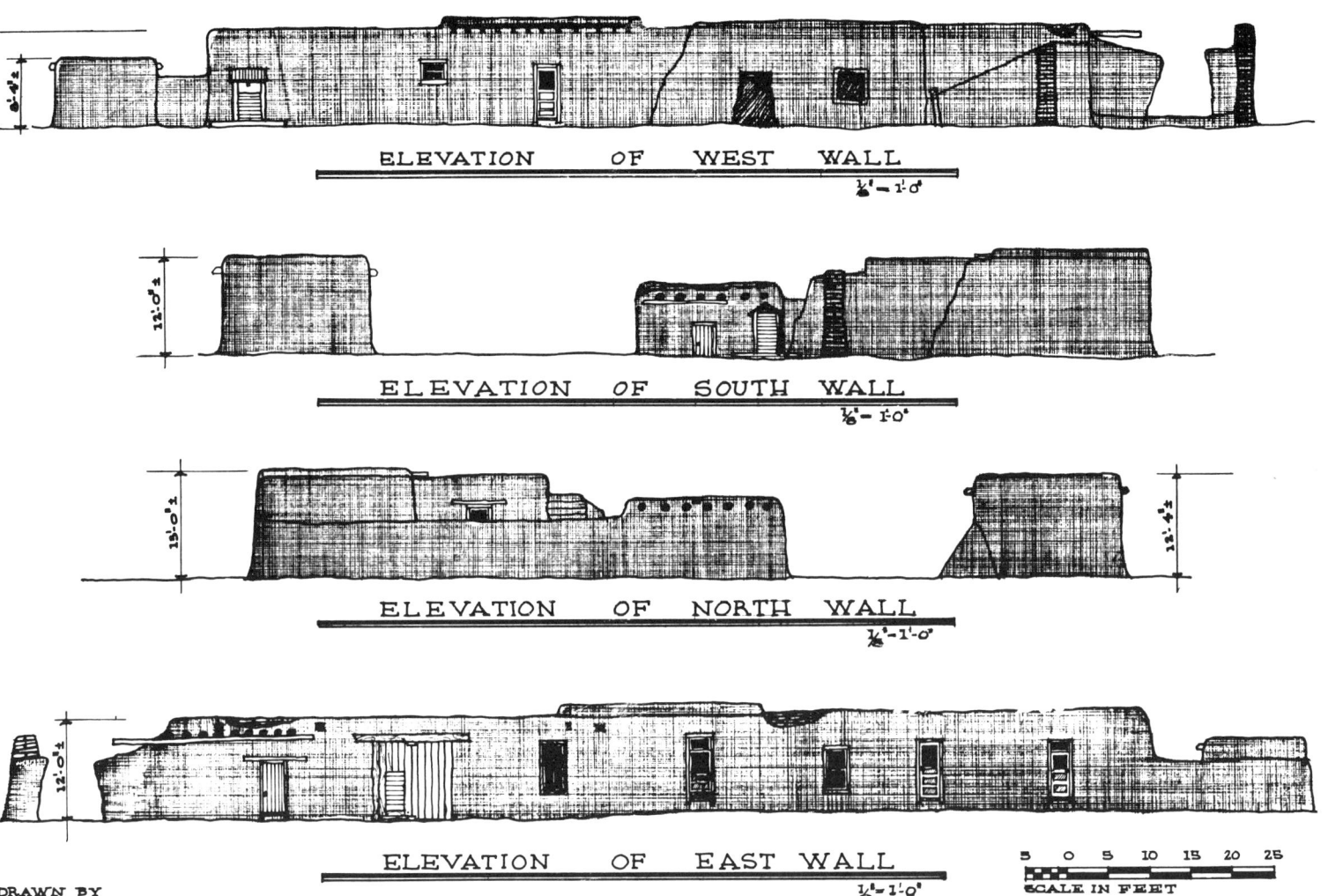

Figure 6. Main elevations showing what remains of the perimeter wall.

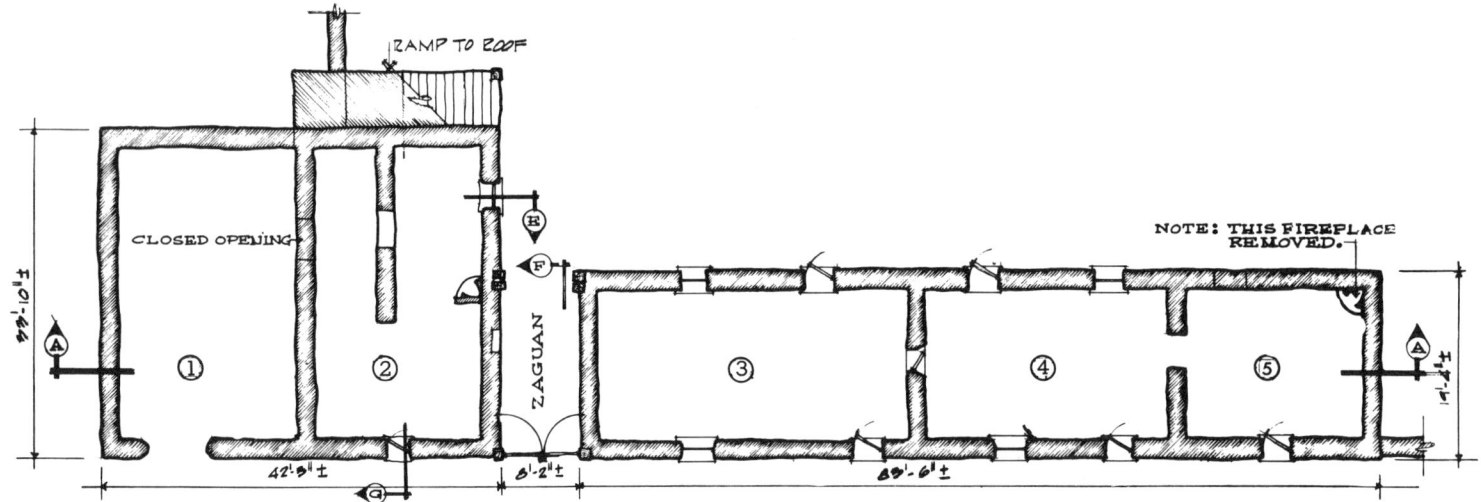

Figure 7. Rooms remaining along east front of house. Room 2 was the cantina; still another room, situated on the extreme right, has disappeared.

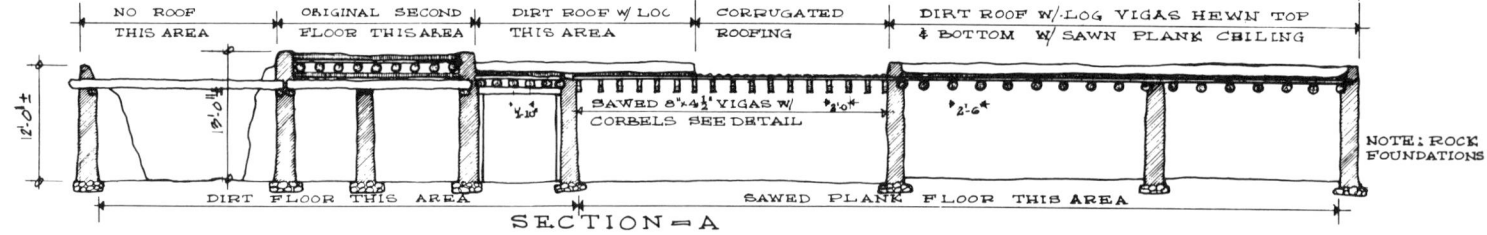

Figure 8. Longitudinal section of rooms shown in Figure 7. Notes indicate type of roof in position in 1961.

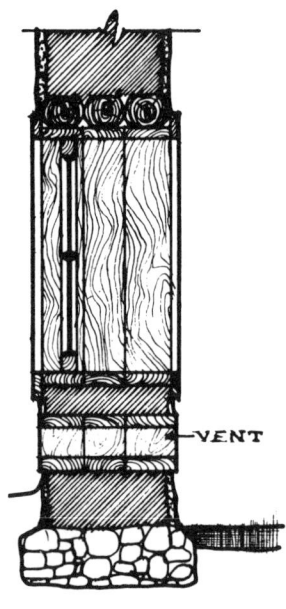

Figure 9. Section of window in cantina. The unusual vented shelf below the window sill may have been a wine cooler.

Figure 10. Exterior of zaguán gate. Photograph HABS, Jack Boucher.

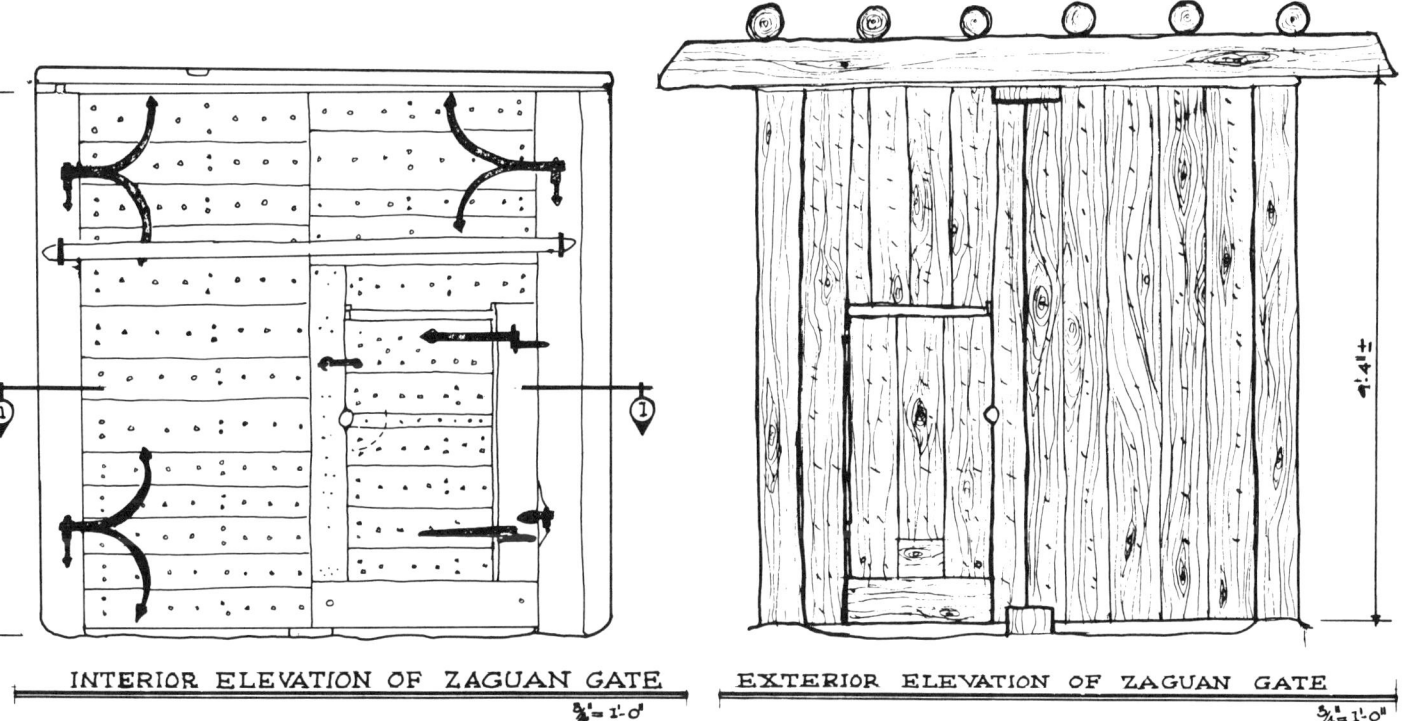

Figure 11. Measured drawing of zaguán gate.

Figure 12. Hand-forged iron hinge of zaguán gate. Photograph HABS, Jack Boucher.

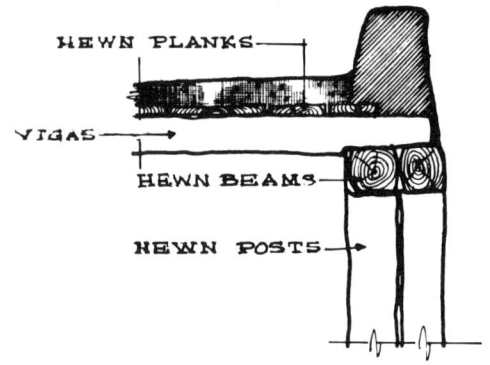

Figure 13. Section of wall above zaguán gate.

Figure 14. Diagram of mortise and tenon of zaguán gate, lintel and jambs.

Figure 15. Cantina fireplace with its deflector wall or "padercito." Photograph HABS, Jack Boucher.

II. Pascual Martinez House
Taos, New Mexico

The Pascuál Martínez house is the best surviving example of a Spanish hacienda in the Taos area. A large structure of considerable architectural interest and for many years unoccupied, it was the home of five generations of the prominent Martínez family. Several unsuccessful attempts were made at rehabilitation in the middle forties. But because the owners do not even live in New Mexico, no one today is protecting it from the devastations of treasure hunters or repairing its leaking roofs.

Situated in the Ranchitos district on the west bank of Taos River about two miles from the Taos Plaza, it is the oldest and largest of a group of three houses in the area owned by the Martínez family—all of which are discussed in the following pages. It was at one time the headquarters of a 10,000 acre ranch, reportedly part of the land grant made in 1788 by the King of Spain to Don Antonio Martínez.

The Martínez family originally lived in Abiquiu, but Don Severino, son of Antonio, gave the Taos property to his son Don Pascuál before the latter's marriage in 1828 to Teodora Gallegos. It is not clear whether Don Severino or Don Pascuál built the house, but both of them lived in it after Don Severino moved to Taos from Abiquiu in 1824.

It is sometimes mistakenly referred to by present-day Taoseños as the Padre Martínez house. This famous priest, a brother of Don Pascuál, did reside in the house with his brother and father for three years after his return to Taos from Mexico in 1826 to assume his clerical duties. His own home, however, was located in the center of Taos.

Don Pascuál Martínez, proprietor of the house under discussion, owned caravans of *carretas* (heavy wooden carts, usually drawn by oxen), which he employed in the Chihuahua trade. He also served in the New Mexico legislature under both the Mexican and United States flags.

Most of the present house was built in 1824, according to the Martínez family historian, Don Leandro Martínez of Santa Fe. A small part of it, however, is much older than that. In the southeast corner, four rooms (10, 11, 13, 14)—earlier formed a separate house. This first small house was purportedly already very old when it was purchased from two Indians in 1824 by Don Severino.

There is a noticeable difference in scale between the original structure and later Martínez additions. The floor level of the Indian part is lower, largely because of the natural slope of the terrain, and the ceiling height is eight feet, as opposed to eleven feet elsewhere (Figure 19). The early rooms are also slightly narrower than those built later, which measure fifteen feet, three inches wide. Today cracks are clearly visible in Room 9 where the walls of the newer buildings join to the old.

From this small beginning the present structure grew. The finished and furnished mansion of twelve rooms was mentioned in an undated newspaper reprint of the marriage festivities of Don Pascuál and Teodora Gallegos in 1828. Except for the later reshuffling of partitions in the original Indian dwelling, the house appears to be much the same today as it was then.

A large, walled service yard and various service buildings were attached to the 90-by-101 foot house at the rear. Only traces of adobe walls from these attachments still exist. At one time a water-powered grist mill stood on the bank of the Taos River in front of the house. Although its date of construction is not known, the mill is shown in a 1901 photograph of the old hacienda (Figure 31).

The patio-centered plan of the enlarged Martínez dwelling is a type common in Spanish lands from Andalusia to Mexico and Peru. Although it is sometimes assumed that all Spanish houses are built about a courtyard, in New Mexico this was only true for a few large haciendas. The three- or four-room houses of the poorer families were too small for such purposes.

The *placita* (patio) of the house is large, 51 x 65 feet, and is approached by an 11-foot entryway, or *zaguán* (Figure 25). Wide enough for a horse-drawn cart, the *zaguán* is entered through heavy double gates of wood (Figure 26). These gates could be securely barred. At the rear of the *placita*, a narrow passage communicates with the *corrál* (stable yard), which was ringed by store rooms, hay barns, chicken house, and carriage house. Originally another double gate and *zaguán* were located on the north side of this service yard. At the front of the *placita* a well stands typically in one corner of the open space, although the little well house has disappeared.

As was fitting in this house of seignorial pretensions, several of the rooms are unusually large. Room 1, thirty-four feet in length, is called the room of Doña Maria. Together with Room 2 it forms a separate apartment. Don Severino was reportedly an independent individual who, as an old man, preferred to live alone. Rooms 5 and 6 were used by Don Juan Manuél Martínez, the last member of the family to reside in the house, as a servant's room and kitchen, but the present dividing partition of adobe appears to be of later construction than the rest of the house.

Featuring two fireplaces (Figure 21), handsome windows, a double door (Figure 24) and a combined length of forty-four feet, the above rooms may originally have served as the *sala* (drawing room) or as the large store room where Don Pascuál kept the goods he imported from Mexico. Room 3 has unusually small corbels, which support the squared beams. Room 7 has apparently always been a store room because of its high, wood-barred window. After the house was enlarged by the Martínez family, the early rooms of Indian construction were used as servants' quarters.

The Spanish families who did not huddle together in tightly grouped communities for mutual protection from the Indians had to defend themselves independently. The Martínez house could be defended, for during its first three or four decades of occupancy it had no exterior openings except the main gateway. The present outside windows and single doors were not cut through until a later time.

In addition to the unbroken circuit of exterior walls, the adobe parapet was originally carried up high enough to protect the guards who on occasion defended the roof tops (Figure 32). Loop-holes (*tronecas*) are said by members of the family to have been cut through these upper walls, but heavy erosion has eliminated any trace of them. A hatchway to the house roof from the patio portal was still in place when the accompanying photographs were taken in 1923 (Figure 20). Approached by a ladder, it opened onto the lower roof of the original Indian rooms.

The appearance of the fortress-like old mansion has been greatly altered during its more than 140 years. A major remodeling was effected about the time of the Civil War. At that time, two single doors and eleven windows, most of them of good size and some equipped with elaborate wood trim, were cut through the exterior walls. Another improvement added a wooden *portál* across the entire ninety-foot facade as well as around all sides of the *placita* (Figures 16, 20, 23, and 24).

The simple design of these *portales*, constructed of rounded rather than squared posts and without capital-like moldings, may indicate an earlier date than the 1862 veranda of the Leandro Martínez house next door (Chapter IV). When the *portál* inside the *placita* was added, however, it blocked the entrance of vehicles into the patio from the *zaguán* (Figure 20). Because easy access to the *placita* was necessary for reasons of defense, this alteration most probably post-dates the establishment of Fort Burgwin in 1853, an event that brought the Indians under control in the Taos area.

The nicely detailed window trim and shutters, still seen in the 1923 photographs, give the appearance of a later date than do the simpler *portales* (Figure 30). The paneled door frame of finished lumber used for the main gates of the house also makes an interesting contrast with the earlier, about 1839, *zaguán* gate of the Horace Long house (Chapter I), which was built of rough adzed logs and featured roughly shaped mortise and tenon joints and forged iron hardware (Figure 14). The relatively large amounts of window-glass in the remodeled Martínez house also indicate a reasonably late date for the windows. Except in the remodeled entryway, Room 13, the house never had wooden floors.

The Martínez family occupied the house until 1926, at which time they moved to a smaller, more practical house down the river a short way. Eventually the property was sold for back taxes. For a while the house was owned by the Taos artist, Martin Shaeffer, who undertook a restoration in 1944. At that time, a portion of the north wall in Room 1 collapsed while workmen were attempting to add a concrete foundation. Instead of rebuilding the wall, the present large window with its overhanging roof was added. After Mr. Shaeffer was forced to suspend restoration, the house changed owners several times, but no further work was done toward structural stabilization.

Because of leaking roofs, pools of water collected in certain rooms, weakening foundations, and causing the walls to sag. Most destructive of all, treasure hunters ransacked the abandoned house. They excavated under every fireplace and in almost every corner. Then groundhogs began undermining the never-too-sturdy foundations. Vandals broke window sash and wind tore off shutters. By 1960 the house had probably deteriorated beyond the point of redemption.

Yet the thick adobe mass still looms over the Taos Plain, a sad remnant of one of the finest haciendas in all of New Mexico.

Figure 16. Main elevation as it appeared about 1923. Photograph courtesy of Mrs. Rowena Martinez.

Figure 17. Main elevation as it appeared in 1962. Photograph HABS, Jack Boucher.

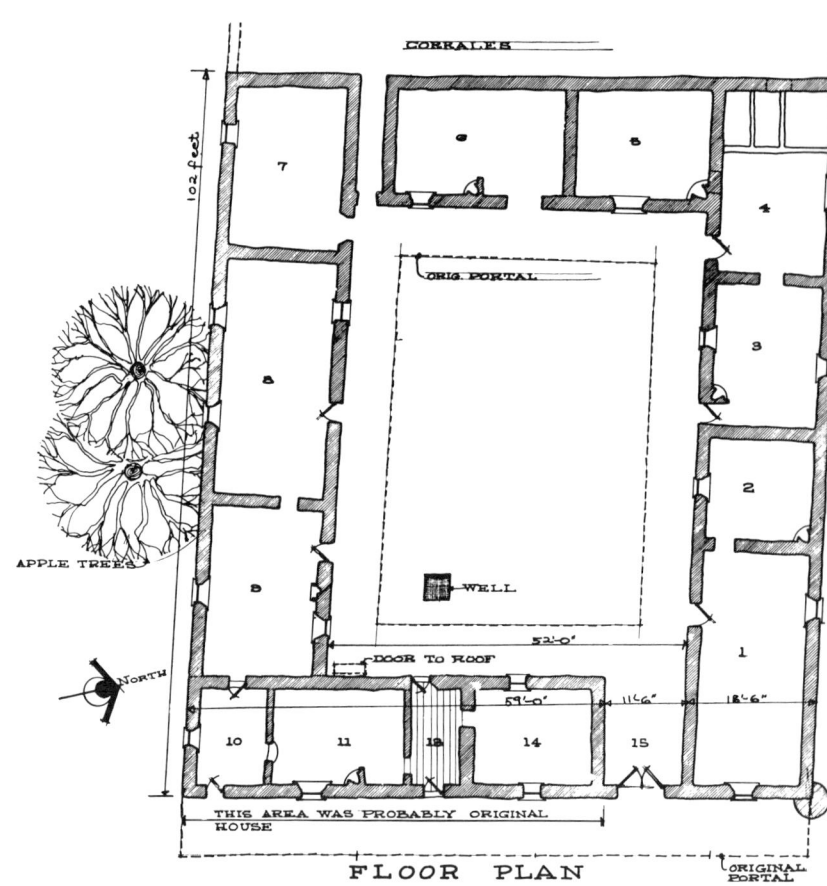

Figure 18. A typical New Mexican hacienda plan with a single file of rooms around a placita. Stable yard and barns abutted on the rear.

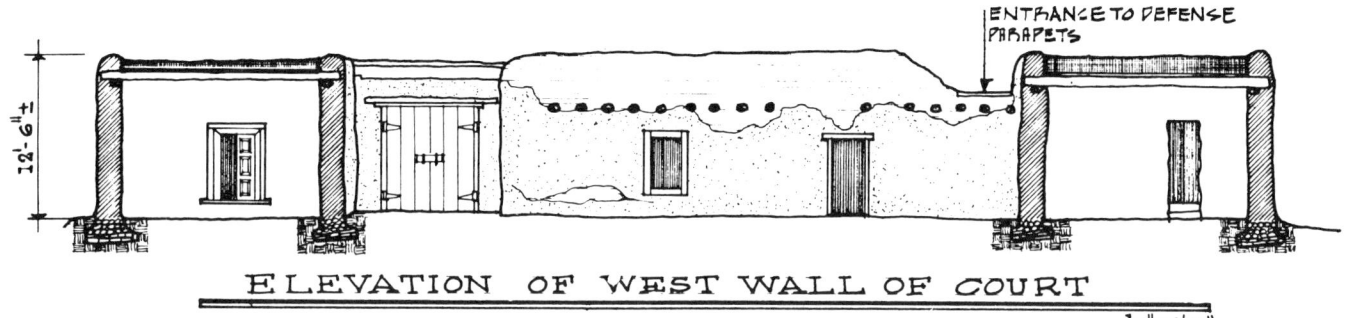
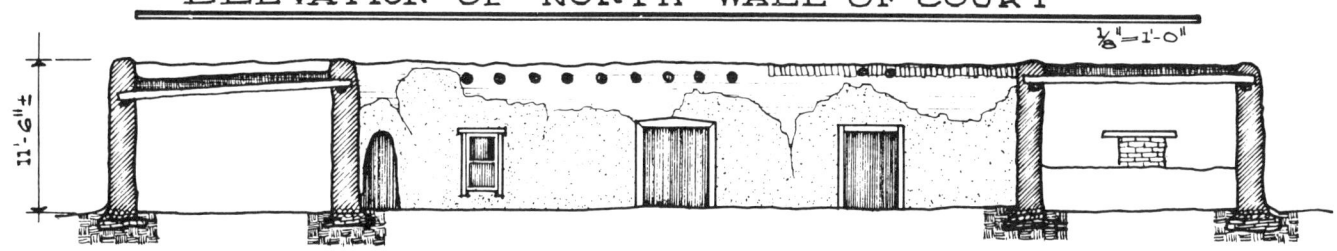
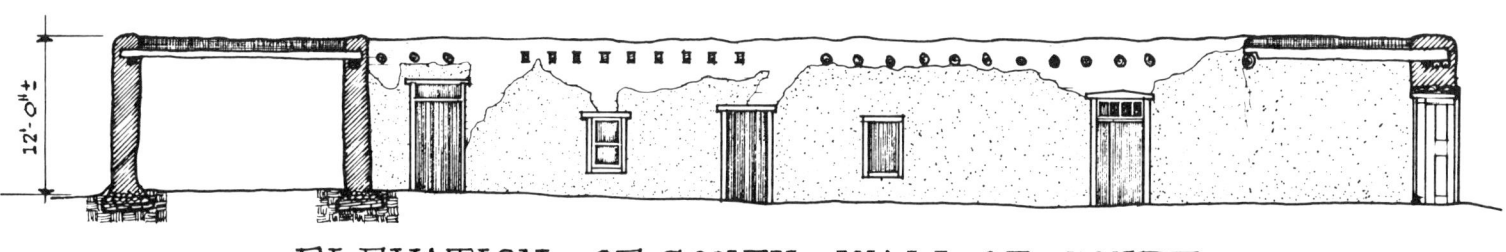

Figure 19. Sections and elevations of the placita.

Figure 20. East wall of the placita as it appeared about 1923; the later portál obstructs passage through the zaguán. Photograph courtesy of Mrs. Rowena Martínez.

Figure 21. Corner fireplace.

Figure 22. Arch to rear passage leading to stable yard. The arch, however, is not structural. Photograph by Roy Boyd.

Figure 23. North wall of placita as it appeared in 1923. The portál was a later addition. Photograph courtesy of Mrs. Rowena Martinez.

Figure 24. West wall of placita as it appeared in 1923. Photograph courtesy of Mrs. Rowena Martinez.

Figure 25. Corner of placita in 1962 showing zaguán and door to sala. Photograph by Roy Boyd.

Figure 26. Zaguán gate from exterior. Photograph HABS, Jack Boucher.

Figure 27. Plan of zaguán gate.

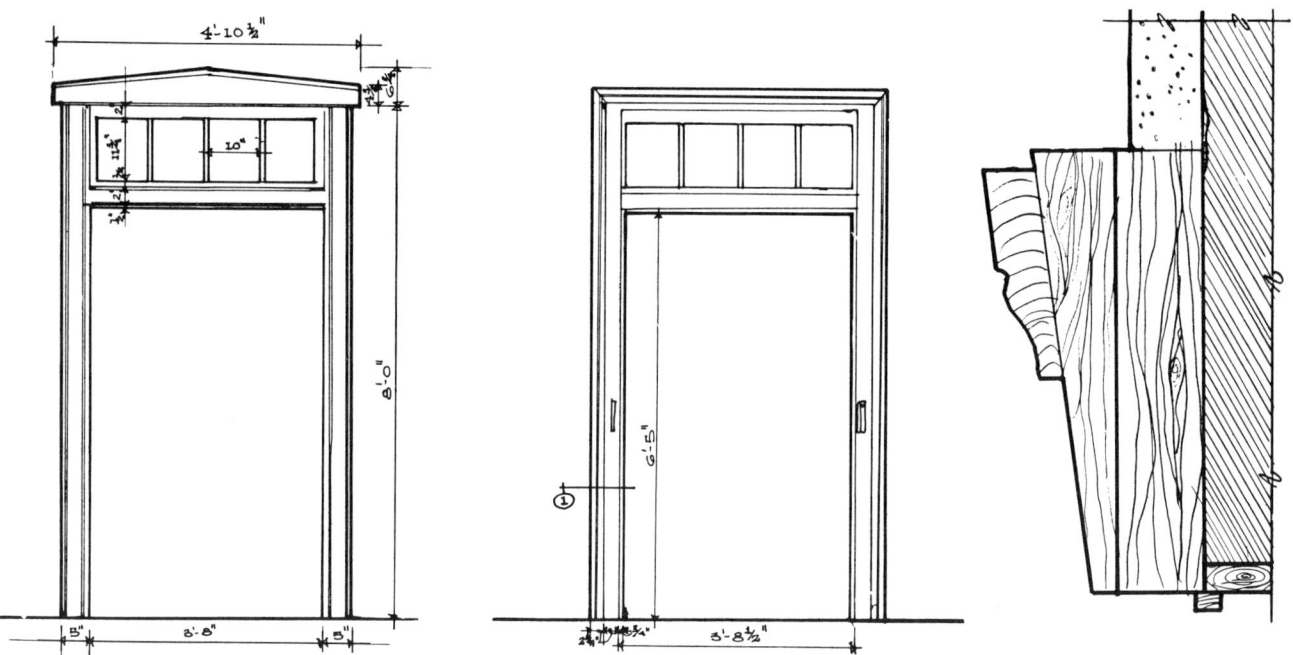

Figure 28. Interior, exterior, and trim detail of door to Room 1.

Figure 29. Northeast corner of placita.

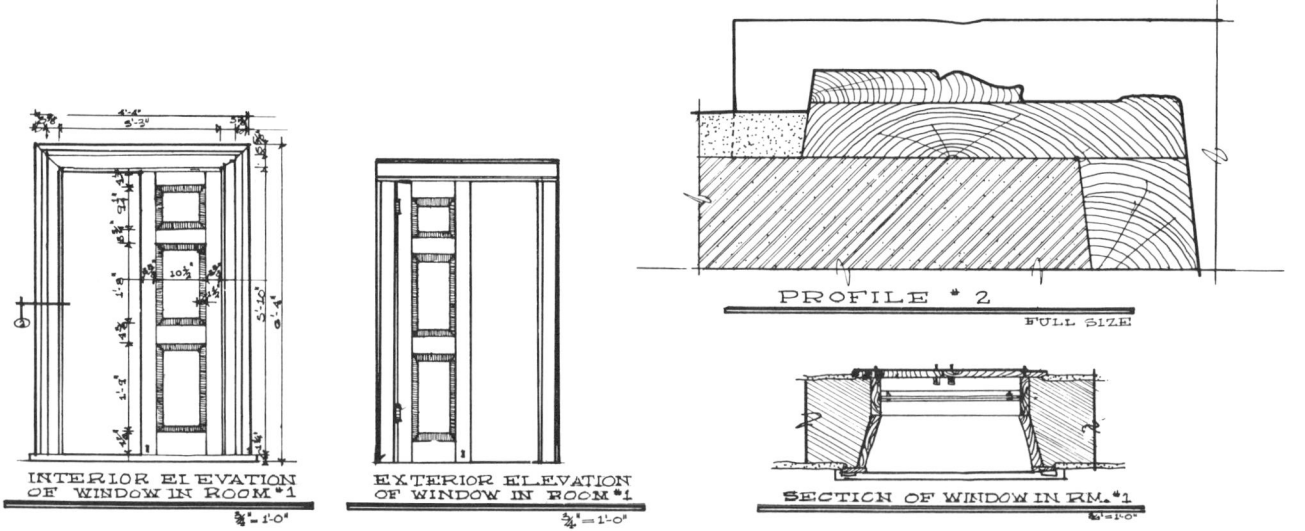

Figure 30. Elevations, plan, and detail of trim for window in Room 1.

Figure 31. Log grist mill in front of the house. It was powered by water from the Taos River. Photograph of 1901 courtesy Mr. Leandro Martinez.

Figure 32. Reconstruction of original appearance of house. The absence of outside windows and the presence of loopholes along the top of the wall indicate the semi-military aspect of such a hacienda. Sketch by Jean Lee Booth.

III. Jose Maria Martinez House
Taos, New Mexico

This house was built about 1833 by Don José Maria Martínez, the second son of Don Severino and a brother of Padre Martínez and of Don Pascuál, whose large hacienda stands just across the Taos River. Don José's house commanded about 1,000 acres east of the river, land which had been a part of the Antonio Martínez estate.

Information regarding the house is scanty because this branch of the family left Taos in 1897 for Wagon Mound, New Mexico. Two living grandnephews of Don José agree substantially on the construction date of the house: Don Juan Manuél Martínez of Taos states that it was built about 1830; and Don Leandro Martínez of Santa Fe, 1833.

Architecturally this house is less interesting than the other two Martínez houses. It is a medium-size, patio-centered house. The *placita,* not large enough to enter with wagon or carriage, has no *zaguán.* The present double entrance doors of Room 7 appear to be a late addition.

In the absence of rooms along the east side of the *placita,* a deep *portál* having a solid exterior wall closes in the area. Built without *zapatas* (corbel brackets), the design of this *portál* is unusually plain (Figure 37). And because of the *placita's* restricted dimensions, the narrow interior *portales* that once ran around the other three sides amounted to little more than covered walkways. Equipped with the usual well, the *placita* was a pleasant area, probably planted with a small garden.

Room 1 has an ingenious window, whose two sets of sash resemble a modern storm window (Figure 38). Such a window, set in an outside wall and made from planed lumber quite intricately molded, can hardly date before the late 1860's. The door and windows in Rooms 3 and 4 are good specimens of handmade sash and frames (Figures 39 and 40).

An old fashioned window barred with iron straps is located in Room 5 apparently always used as a store room. Such a window, high, narrow, and lacking glass, is the type probably used in New Mexico prior to 1865, except that the use of iron dates it later.

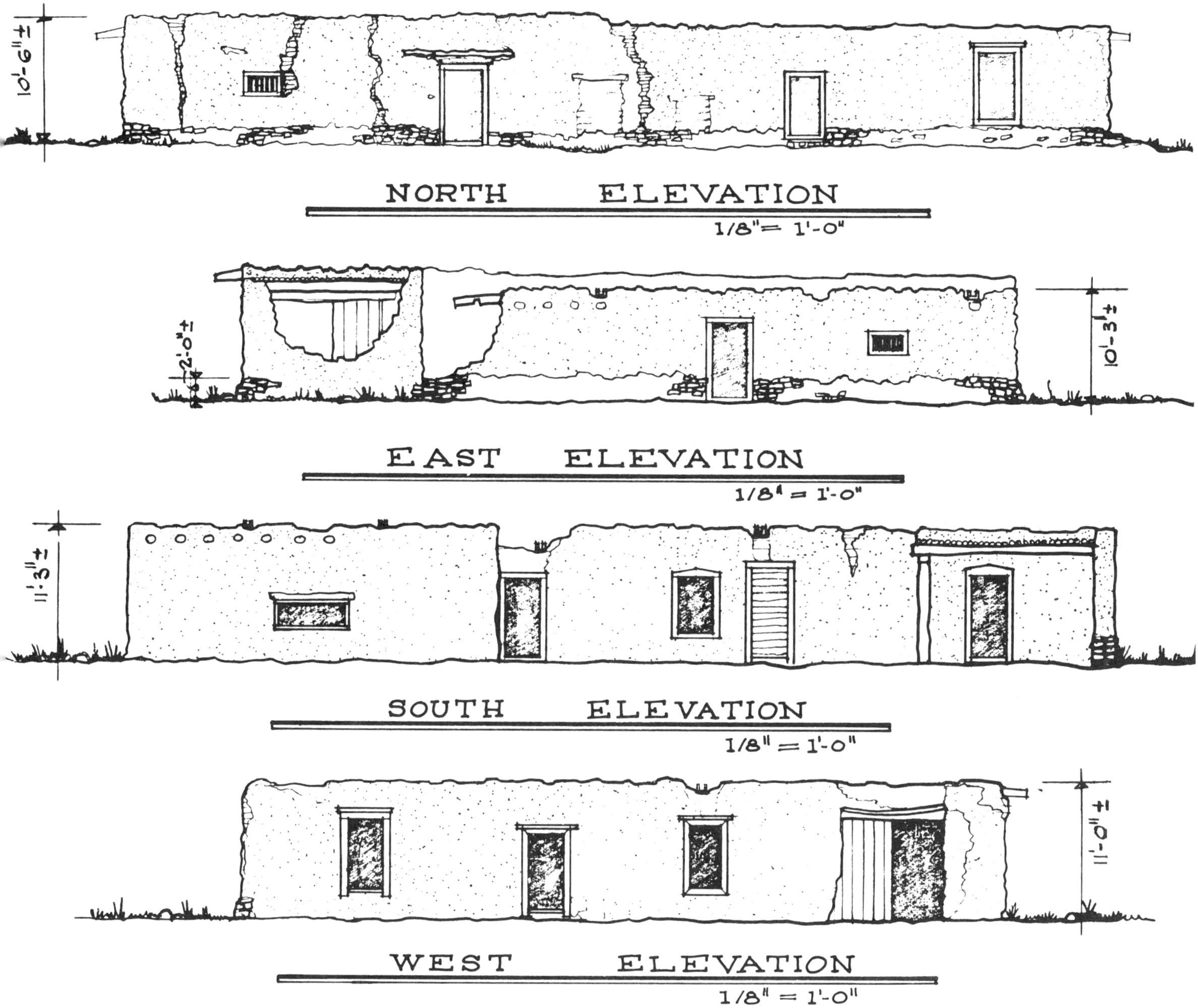
10'-6"±
NORTH ELEVATION
1/8" = 1'-0"
2'-0"±
10'-3"±
EAST ELEVATION
1/8" = 1'-0"
11'-3"±
SOUTH ELEVATION
1/8" = 1'-0"
11'-0"±
WEST ELEVATION
1/8" = 1'-0"

Figure 33. Main elevations.

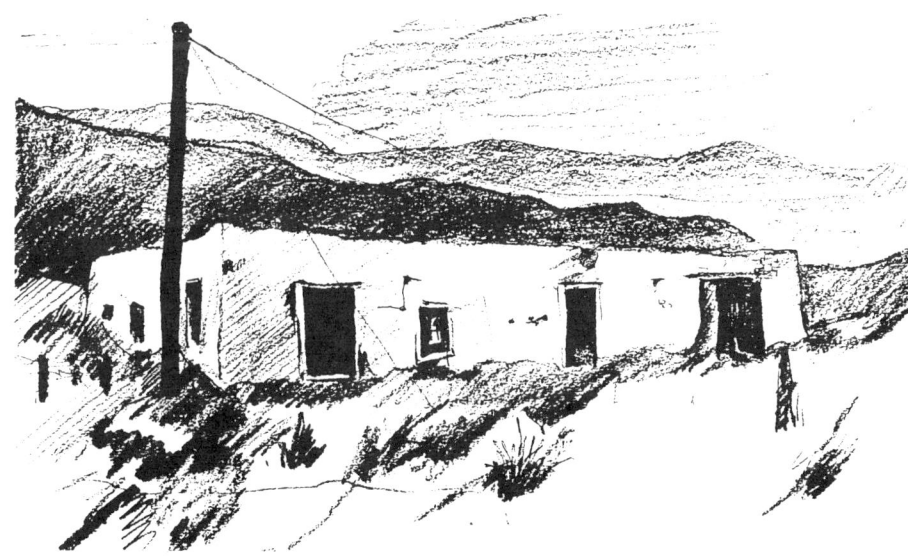

Figure 34. West facade. Sketch by Jean Lee Booth.

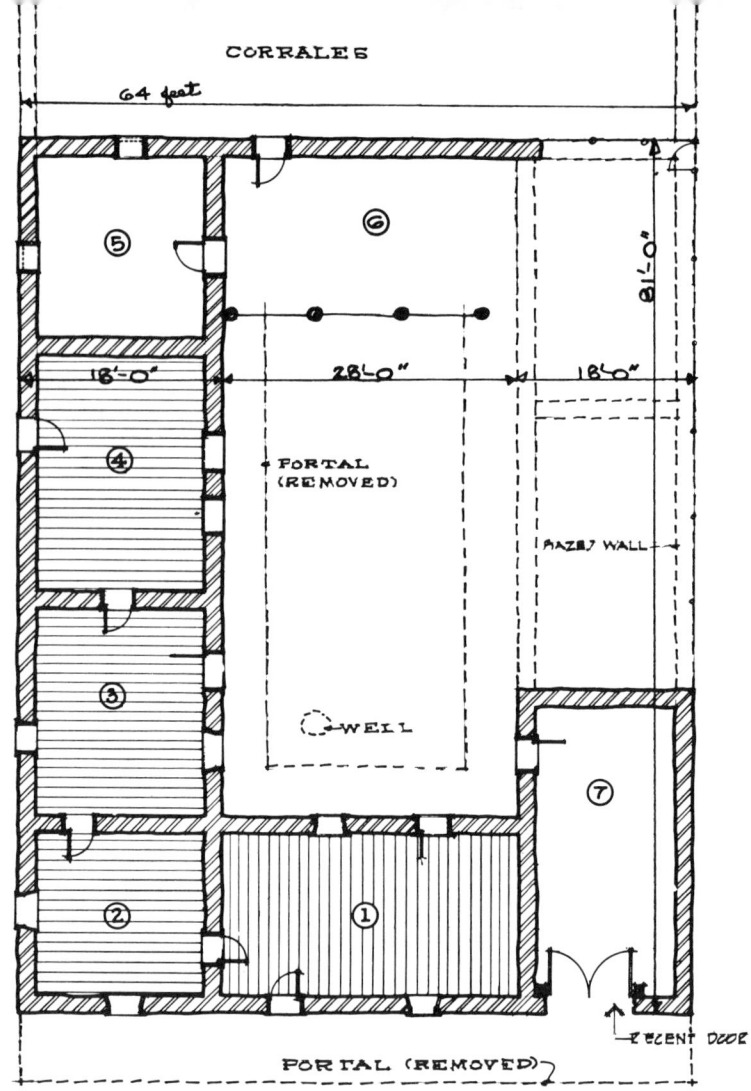

FLOOR PLAN
1/8" = 1'-0"

Figure 35. Plan.

Figure 36. Remaining portál. Sketch by Jean Lee Booth.

Figure 37. Northwest corner of placita. Sketch by Jean Lee Booth.

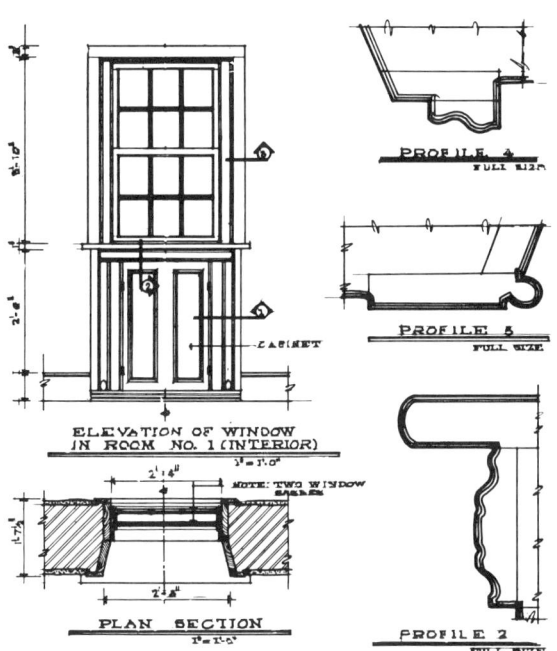

Figure 38. Details of window in Room 1. The double sash and cabinet below are unusually elaborate millwork.

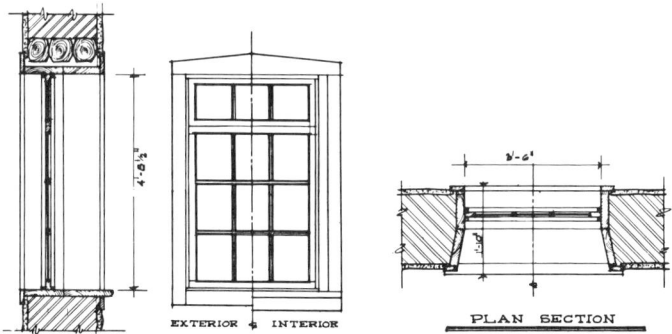

Figure 39. Details of window in Room 3.

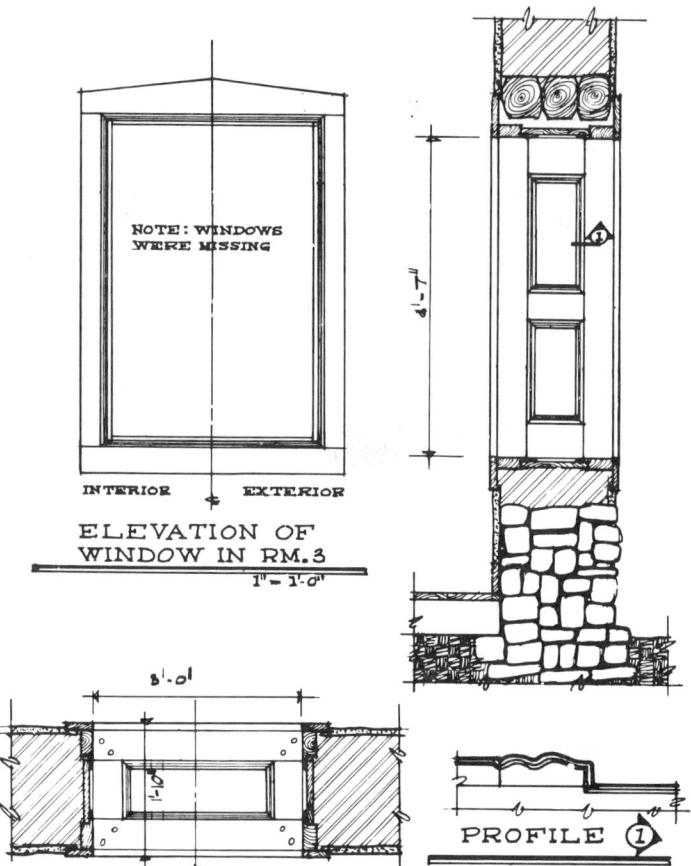

Figure 40. Details of window in Room 4.

Figure 41. Interior doorway between Rooms 1 and 2. Sketch by Jean Lee Booth.

IV. Leandro Martínez House
Taos, New Mexico

The Leandro Martínez house, the third of the three Martínez dwellings in the Ranchitos district near Taos, stands adjacent to the Pascuál Martínez home on the north. Born in 1834, Leandro was the youngest son of Don Pascuál, and like his father, was engaged in commerce. Whereas Pascuál extended his trading expeditions to Chihuahua after 1835, Leandro's *carretas* lumbered to and from St. Louis after 1862, an indication of the new economic orientation of New Mexico in the 1850's and 1860's and one which helps to explain the striking architectural differences between the two houses.

Built in 1862, the Leandro Martínez house is a splendid example of Territorial architecture and is radically different in plan and appearance from the traditional Spanish Colonial architecture of New Mexico. Instead of the single file of rooms—whether in a straight line, in an L-shape, or about a *placita* —the rooms are here placed two deep along a center hall (Figure 45). The plan is rigorously symmetrical, and a wide veranda extends across the facade as an integral part of the design.

Throughout the house the wood trim is made from carefully planed boards, and the woodwork of the principal rooms is joined and paneled with a precision unusual in nineteenth-century New Mexico. The *portál* and the frames of the main entrance and two front windows are particularly elaborate. Unfortunately, the original front doors had been removed before the accompanying photographs were made.

The *portál* bears clear evidence of an important technological advance in Taos as well as a new fashion in architecture (Figure 43). The squared eight-inch wooden posts, having chamfered corners are obviously mill-sawn. They are exact duplicates of those on the *portál* of the Galeria Escondida in Taos, a building known to have been remodeled in 1860. The posts for both buildings probably were cut at the Six Mile Creek sawmill, which was established about that time.

The roof of the *portál,* as the old photographs of 1901 indicate, was once treated like a classical entablature, but the upright posts lack the wooden moldings that usually recalled the Classical capital and base. Such conceits as the entablature and posts clearly indicate that the old Greek Revival style, so long popular in the eastern United States, was at last arriving on the western frontier. The typical classical emphasis on balance and order are obvious in the central hall plan and the rigorously symmetrical disposition of the main facade. This house is certainly the best surviving example of Territorial architecture in the Taos area.

Don Leandro was, according to his son, an avid carpenter as well as a successful merchant. Between his trading expeditions to St. Louis he busied himself with carpentry, more as a hobby than a necessity. The son, Don Leandro Martínez, Jr., now living in Santa Fe, credits his father with the construction of all of the wood trim, including that on the *portál*. He also reports that his father sometimes fashioned windows or doors for the houses of friends in Taos. He says that the date 1862 was once penciled in the ceiling on the south end of the *portál*.

The *portál* is a delightful bit of nineteenth-century architectural whimsy. The bannister that once ran between the veranda posts was of a very simple design (Figure 42). If it had been built a few years later, the balusters would undoubtedly have been more elaborate. The simple balustrade contrasts with the ingenious jigsaw work of the facia at the eave line.

The facia of the little open chapel in Peñas Negras cemetery, a mile south of the Martínez houses, is cut to the same design. Although the present facia is a replica made in 1960, the original facia, according to his son, was done by Don Leandro.

Leandro was probably strongly influenced by the buildings that he observed on his trading trips to St. Louis. Measurements of his house reveal a degree of care and accuracy in layout and construction that is highly unusual in rural New Mexico. Right angles actually measure 90 degrees; walls are of uniform thickness and always plumb; windows and doors are centered accurately. Unusually thick walls—in some place thirty-two inches—suggest that Don Leandro may have contemplated a second story for his house.

Two-story houses featuring a double-decked veranda were common in Missouri, and sometimes, in the pursuit of prestige, they were copied in New Mexico. The hypothesis of an intended second story is strengthened by the presence in the Leandro Martínez house of an unusually heavy hallway ceiling beam in line with the back walls of the two parlors. This beam would be meaningless structurally if not placed there to support an upper story.

The width of the center hall also suggests the intention of an additional story. Eight-feet, ten inches wide, the hall is more than sufficient for a corridor but not quite wide enough for a *sala*, sometimes used in houses of this period. It would, however, have been wide enough to accommodate an ample stairway and passage.

The neglect and deterioration of this artistic landmark is as sad as that of the Pascuál Martínez house. Abandoned since the early 1940's, the terneplate roof long preserved the house from too rapid decay. The roof of Room 4, however, was badly deteriorated by 1960 and the ground hogs had begun their excavations. The *portál*, at that time, was still in a fair state of preservation. In the autumn of 1962, the remaining woodwork was purchased and removed by Larry Frank for his remodeling of the Upper Morada at Arroyo Hondo (Chapter VII).

Figure 42. Main facade as it appeared in 1901. Photograph courtesy of Mr. Leandro Martínez.

Figure 43. Built in 1862, the scroll work was done by the owner. Photograph HABS, by Jack Boucher.

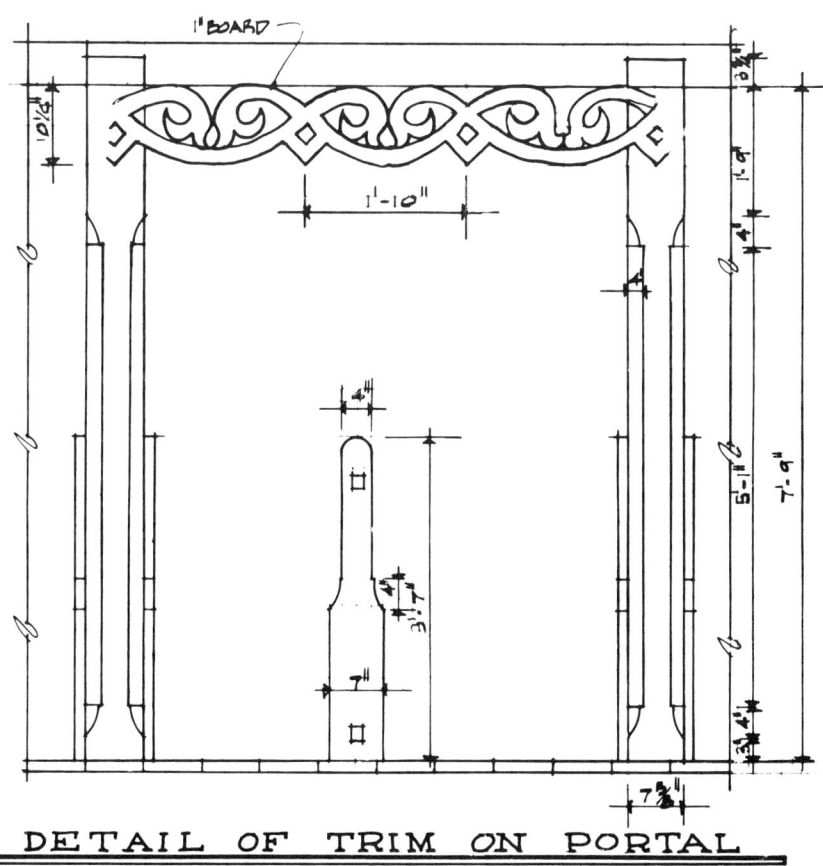

Figure 44. Detail of portal.

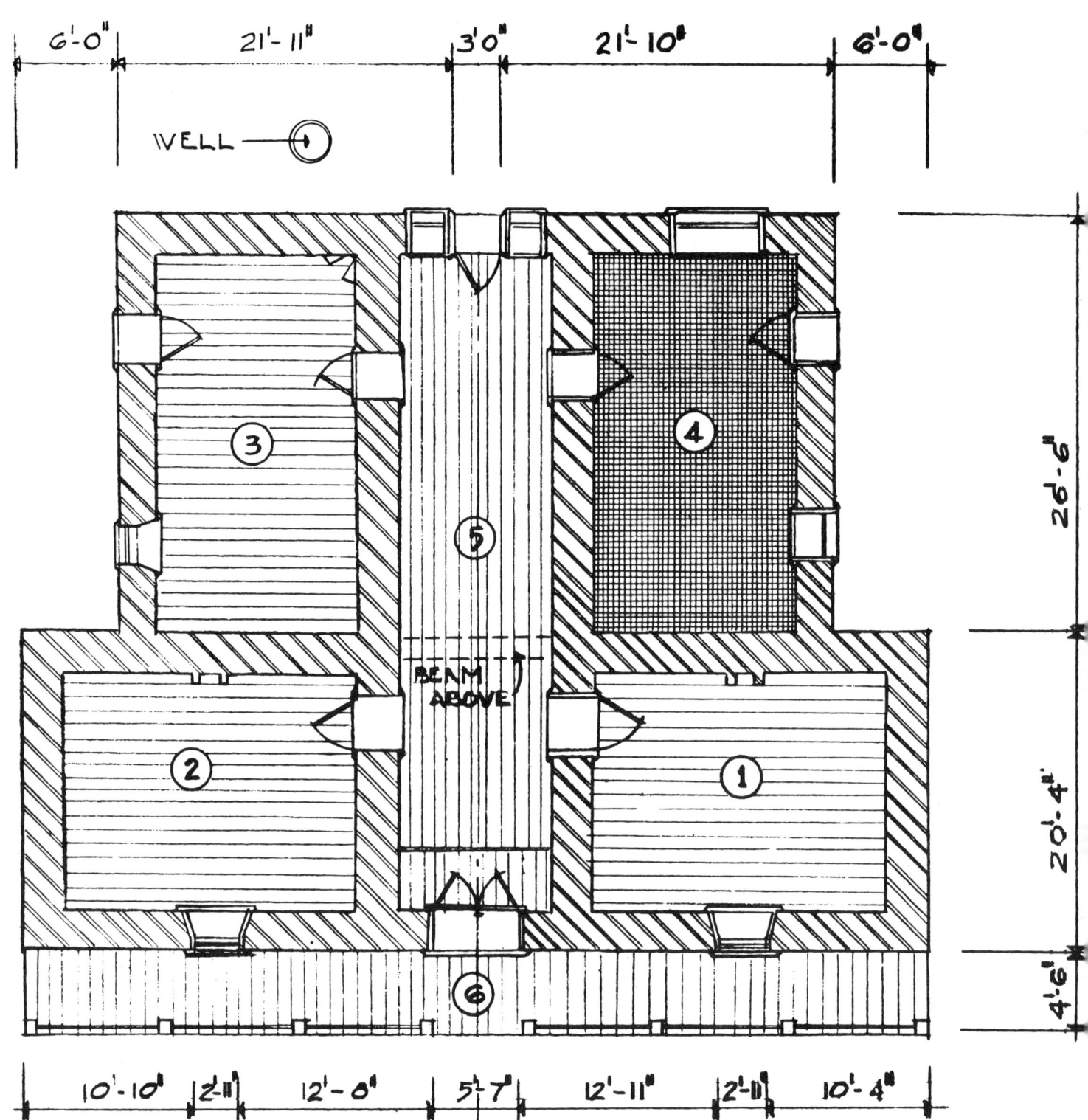

Figure 45. Plan. The more formal center hall plan and doubling of rooms is due to influence of Greek Revival movement.

Figure 46. Sketch of portál by Jean Lee Booth.

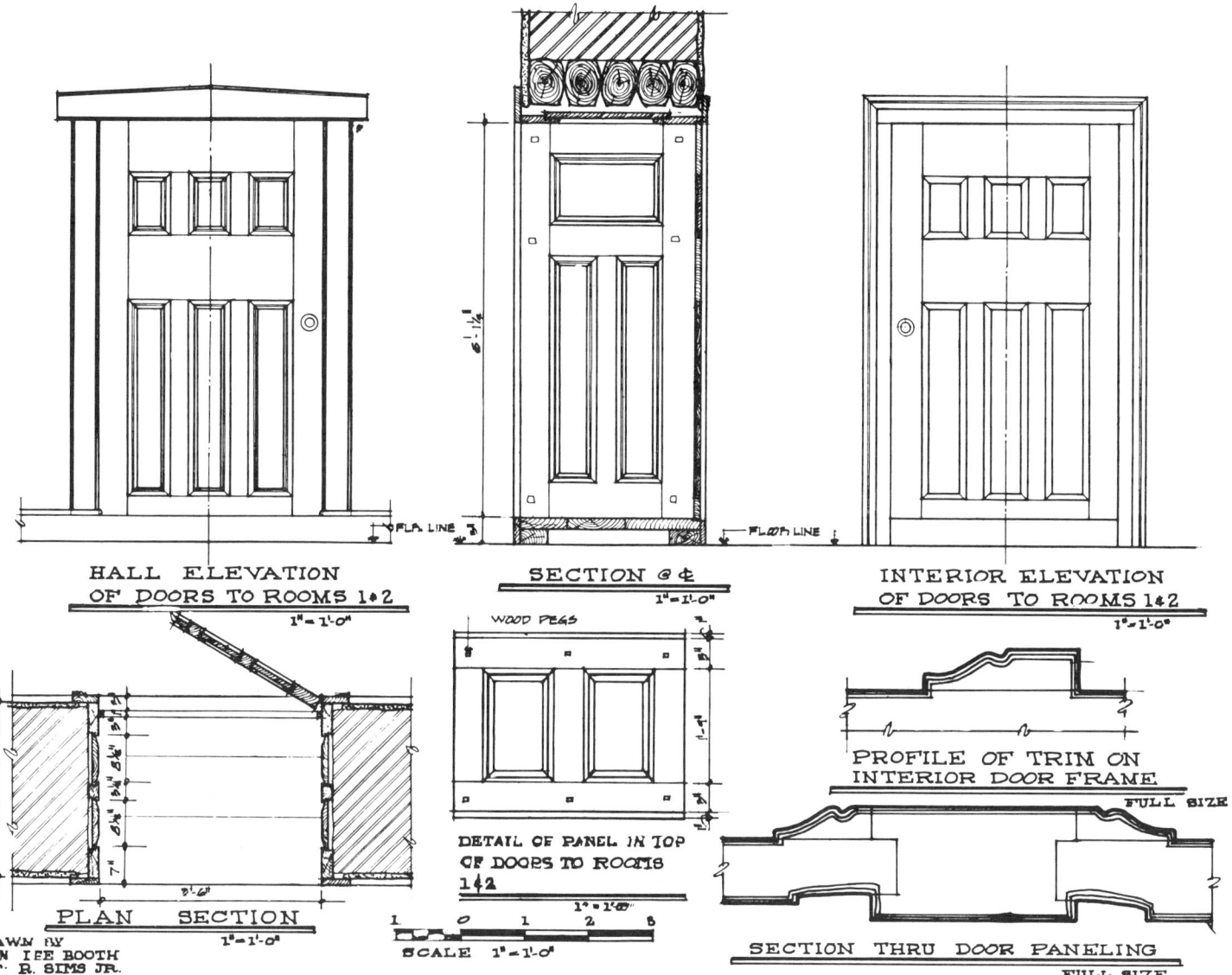

Figure 47. Details of hall doors into Rooms 1 and 2.

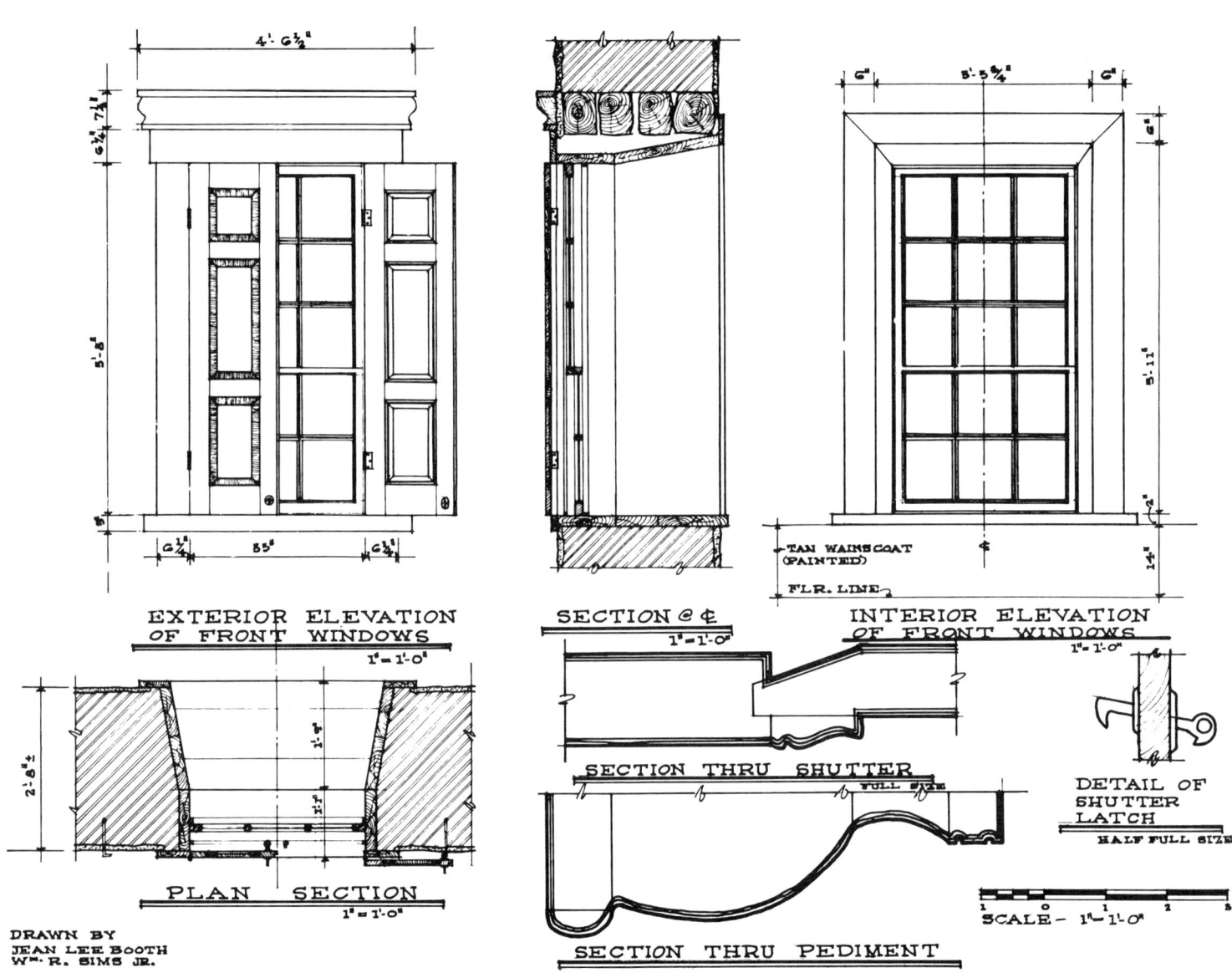

Figure 48. Details of window pictured in Figure 43.

V. Jose Gregorio Valdez House

Taos, New Mexico

The José Gregorio Valdéz house, in the Lomita district of Taos, is a remarkably good example of Spanish Colonial architecture. It is owned today by two unrelated families. The most interesting portion of the old mansion is owned by Mrs. Dewey Struck, a descendent of the Valdéz-Martinez family. Mrs. Struck's portion of the house, Rooms 1, 2, 3, 4 and 12, preserves a splendid Colonial *portál* and a rare over-size fireplace. Rooms 5-11, today abandoned, were originally an integral part of the Valdéz house.

The exact date of construction is unknown. However, Jacob Bernál, long-time resident of Ranchos de Taos and secretary of the Taos Historical Society, believes it is 1834. The Struck family remembers the presence of a date painted on the ceiling of Room 3, which was recently covered with insulation board and cannot therefore be verified. The Strucks think the date was 1806. Of the two dates, 1834 seems more plausible.

Another old inhabitant of Taos and a relation of the family, Isaac Romero, dates the building "from the time" of the Pascuál Martínez house, i.e. 1824. Everyone agrees, however, that the builder was José Gregorio Valdéz and that it was later inherited by his son-in-law, Davíd Martínez, whose name is sometimes attached to it.

Both the *portál* and fireplace are unique, and it is indeed fortunate that they have been so well preserved by the owners. The engineering of the *portál* is as original as it is non-functional (Figure 53). The ceiling of *tablas* (hewn boards) and earth fill is carried by debarked *vigas*, which are supported on the outside by a very stout *umbrál* or lintel. This *umbrál*, which runs the full twenty-foot, eight-inch length of the porch, is a single beam. The remarkable thing about it, however, is that both beam and its *zapatas* (corbel brackets) are cut from the same piece of wood (Figure 54).

Starting with a fourteen inch beam, the outlines of the four *zapatas* were cut free and the three spans between them were cut back to an eight-inch depth. Thus, where the bending moment of the beam was greatest and where, therefore, the greatest depth was required—in the middle of each span—it was actually thinnest (8 inches). It would have been so much easier and more efficient to have cut the *zapatas* from separate, smaller pieces of wood and then laid a beam across the top of the *zapatas*. Not only would it have saved labor in cutting, but a much smaller log would have sufficed.

The faces of the four *zapatas* are decorated with a simple design—a series of incisions, gouged out with a concave chisel. Carved work of this kind, called *evanista* by the Spanish, was less rare in the eighteenth century, when it was used in a number of churches, than in the nineteenth.

The large *fogón de campana*, or bell-shaped fireplace, in Room 2 is unique for several reasons (Figure 51). Even old-time residents of Taos do not remember comparable twin-opening construction. Each of the openings is more than three feet wide, and connects with the fire box. Forms as elaborately sculptural as this are rare in New Mexico, as is also the intricate experimentation in arch construction.

The ceiling in Room 1, the outside wall of which recently collapsed, is of hewn *tablas*. Similar *tablas*, now obscured by insulation board, are reported to be in place in Room 3 and to bear the 1806 (?) inscription.

In terms of existing walls, it is evident that the

house wrapped around the patio on three sides. But, because the building did not extend entirely across the fourth side, the courtyard would undoubtedly have been referred to as a *plazuela* rather than a *placita*. The owners report that in the not-too-distant-past a double gate offered access to the *plazuela* in that section of the north wall which had no rooms behind it.

Although the Struck family can remember no such arrangement, it is quite possible that the house once contained yet another file of rooms completely across the north side of the *plazuela,* similar to the arrangement that still exists in Rooms 5-10 on the south side. This possibility is suggested by the presence of a low terrace of earth about six inches high and fifteen feet wide that runs the whole length of the house in this area.

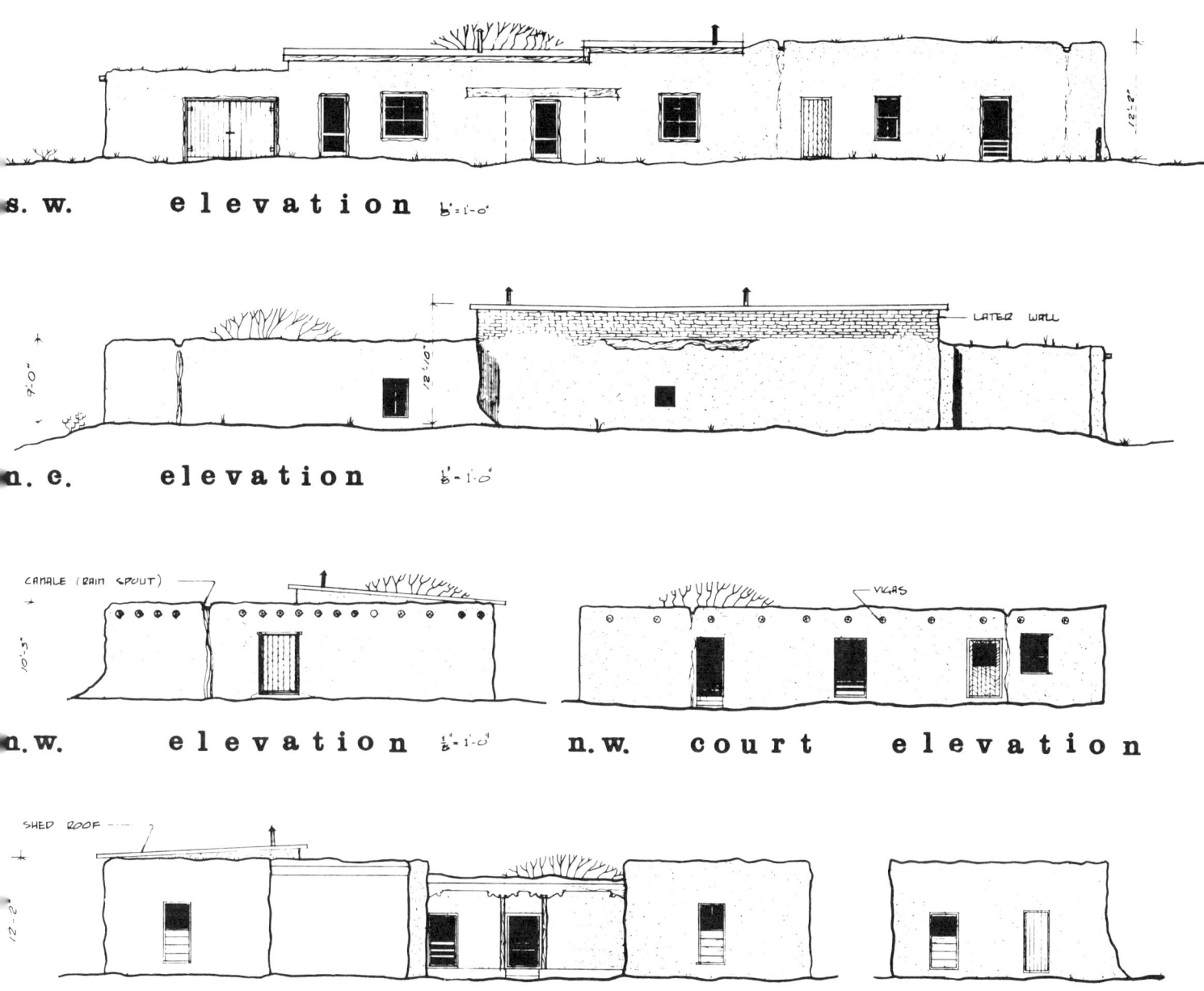

Figure 49. Elevations of house and plazuela. Drawings for this house by George Bales, David Bliss, and Reginald Richey.

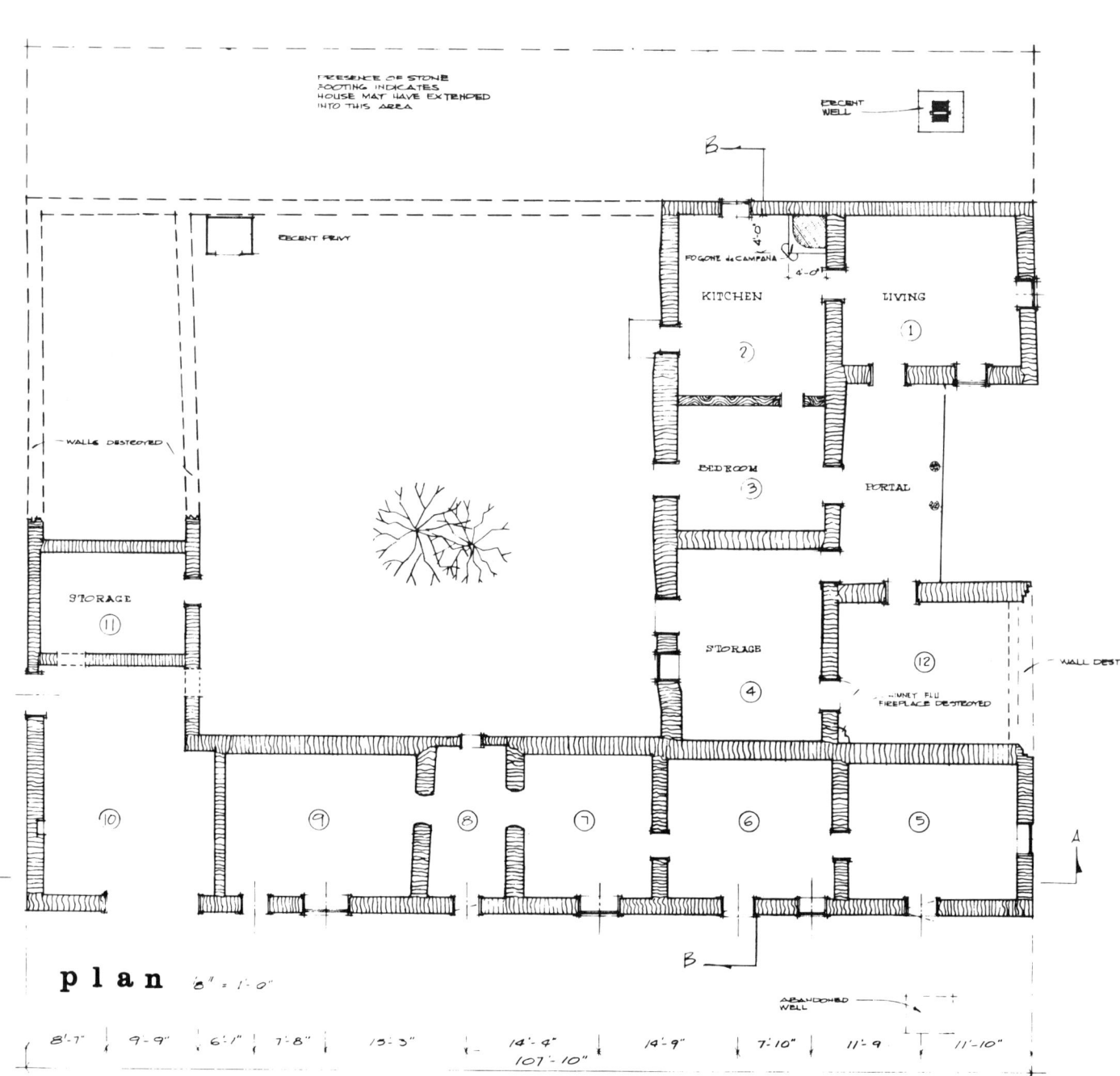

Figure 50. Plan. Subdivided into two separate dwellings today, this house probably consisted of many more rooms than now remain.

Figure 51. Fogón de campana is unique among surviving fireplaces of colonial New Mexico.

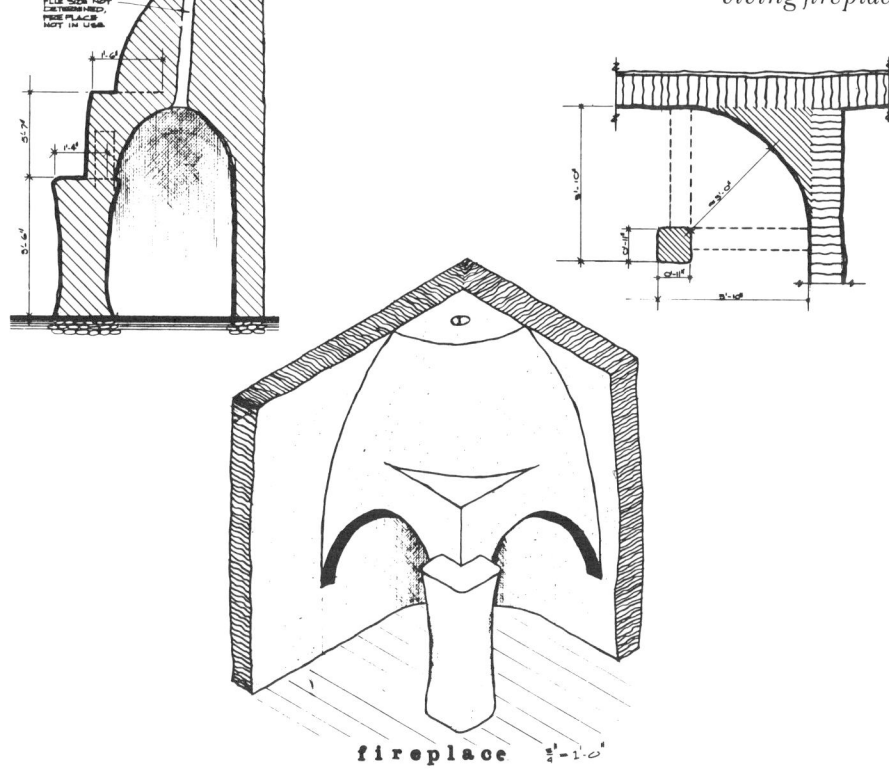

Figure 52. Details of fogón de campana.

Figure 53. The lintel of this elaborate portál is carved from one beam.

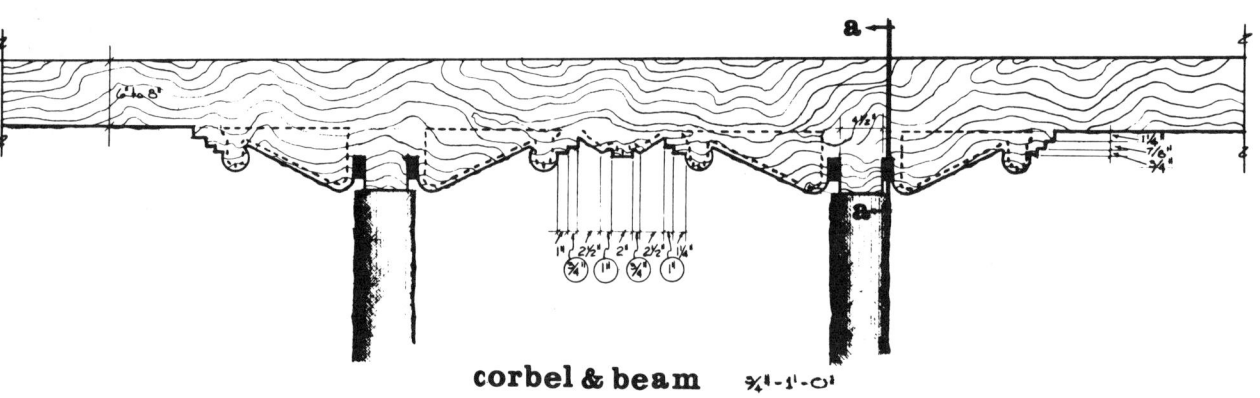

Figure 54. Detail of portál lintel.

VI. Sofio Fernandez House
Llano Quemado, New Mexico

Near the top of the hill and just across the road from the church in Llano Quemado stands the Sofio Fernandez house. Long and casually strung together, abandoned, even the ownership of parts of it unknown, this is hardly a house to catch the visitor's eye; and, save for one striking interior feature—a unique fireplace—is probably not too important.

As with the majority of old New Mexico houses, little factual history is known. But from the vague memories of family descendants and neighbors a partial history of the house can be reconstructed.

The existing U-shaped compound consists of three separate and non-communicating apartments. Rooms 9-14, built perhaps as recently as the 1920's, are quite devoid of interest. Rooms 1-3 were built before World War I by the father of Sofio Fernandez, the present owner of this portion. The conventional fireplace in Room 3, placed against a flat wall and its chimney-breast projecting into the room, represents quite clearly an "Anglo" influence. It was actually built later than Rooms 1-3 by the wife of the present owner of this portion.

The third apartment in this compound, Rooms 4-8, is reported by Sr. Fernandez to be "very, very old." The rooms of this apartment string out in the usual informal fashion and its walls are punctured by an assortment of windows and doors. Room 8 contains an exceedingly interesting and now very rare *fogón*, or fireplace (Figures 56 and 59), apparently the only surviving one of its type in the Taos area.

The fireplace is formed by a stout hand-hewn beam that runs the entire eleven-foot length of the room. At one end, the beam supports a smoke hood, constructed of the same thin (2½ inch) adobe brick normally used in those days for regular chimney flues. A shelf of hewn planks runs the remainder of the beam's length. There is no well-defined firebox because the fire was merely built under the smoke hood, on the floor. On the rear wall is a hole—too small for an oven—that must have served as a warming niche.

Two contradictory explanations are made for the use of this *fogón*, both of which seem plausible. Some hold that it was used as a "shepherd's bed" (see Introduction). Others, however, say that it represented the usual kitchen fireplace arrangement. Mr. Jacob Bernál, the Taos historian, says that he does not remember seeing the shelf being used for a bed, but that prior to the advent of iron cooking stoves this kind of *fogón* was used in many kitchens. The shelf was used for storage. Another interesting feature of Room 8 is a long hewn shelf that runs its entire length and is supported on the end wall.

Sr. Fernandez, owner of the front apartment, says that the old middle apartment (Rooms 4-8) was once part of a large compound formed by it and several adjacent houses. Most of this early complex has fallen into ruins and completely disappeared, while the surviving fragments, like these rooms, have been added to in different directions to form separate houses. Such is the history of New Mexico's organic adobe architecture—a continuing process of decay and growth.

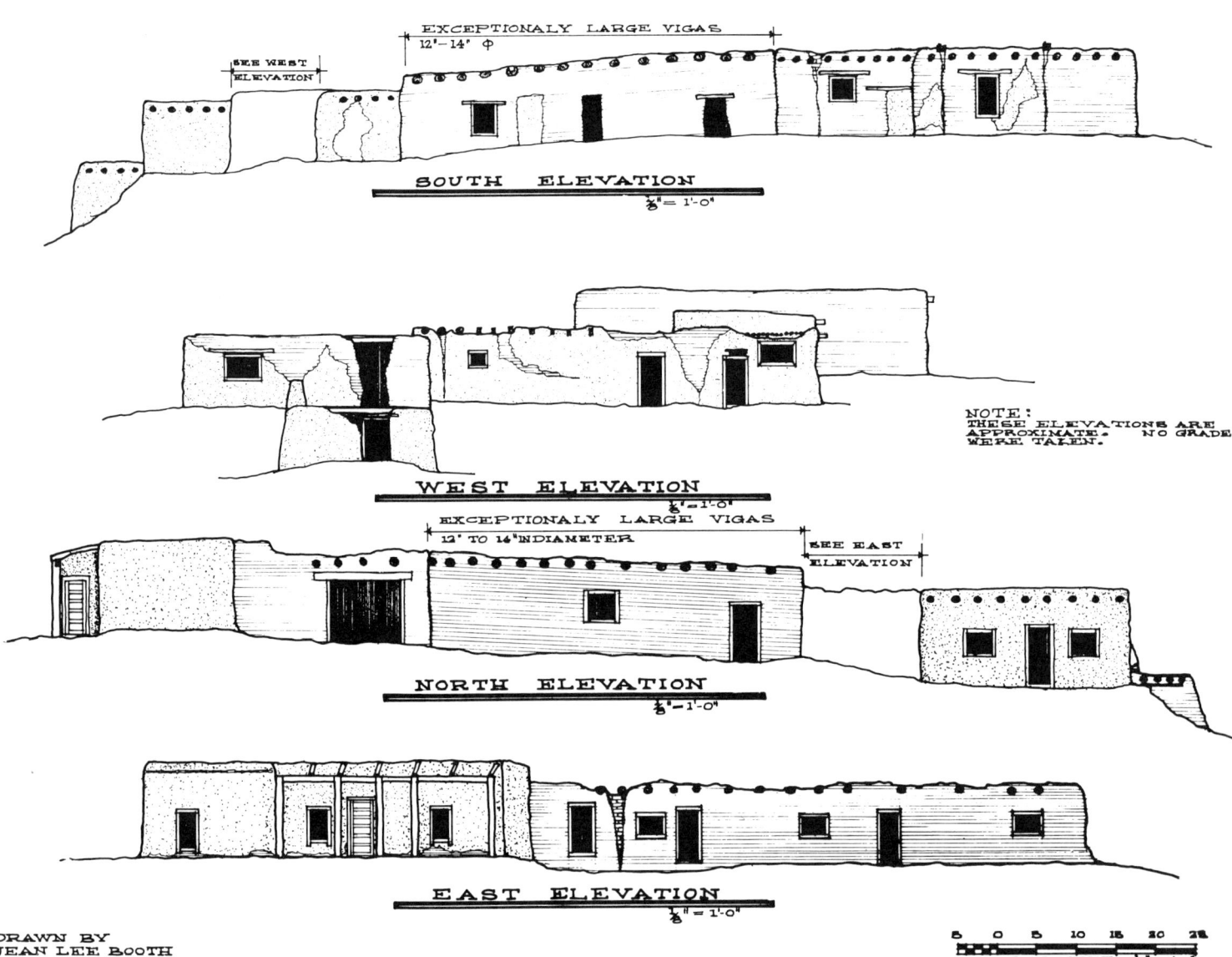

Figure 55. Elevations.

Figure 56. Early New Mexican kitchen fireplace. The fire was built on the floor in a corner. The shelf supported by the long wooden beam was for storage but could also serve as a bed. Photograph by Roy Boyd.

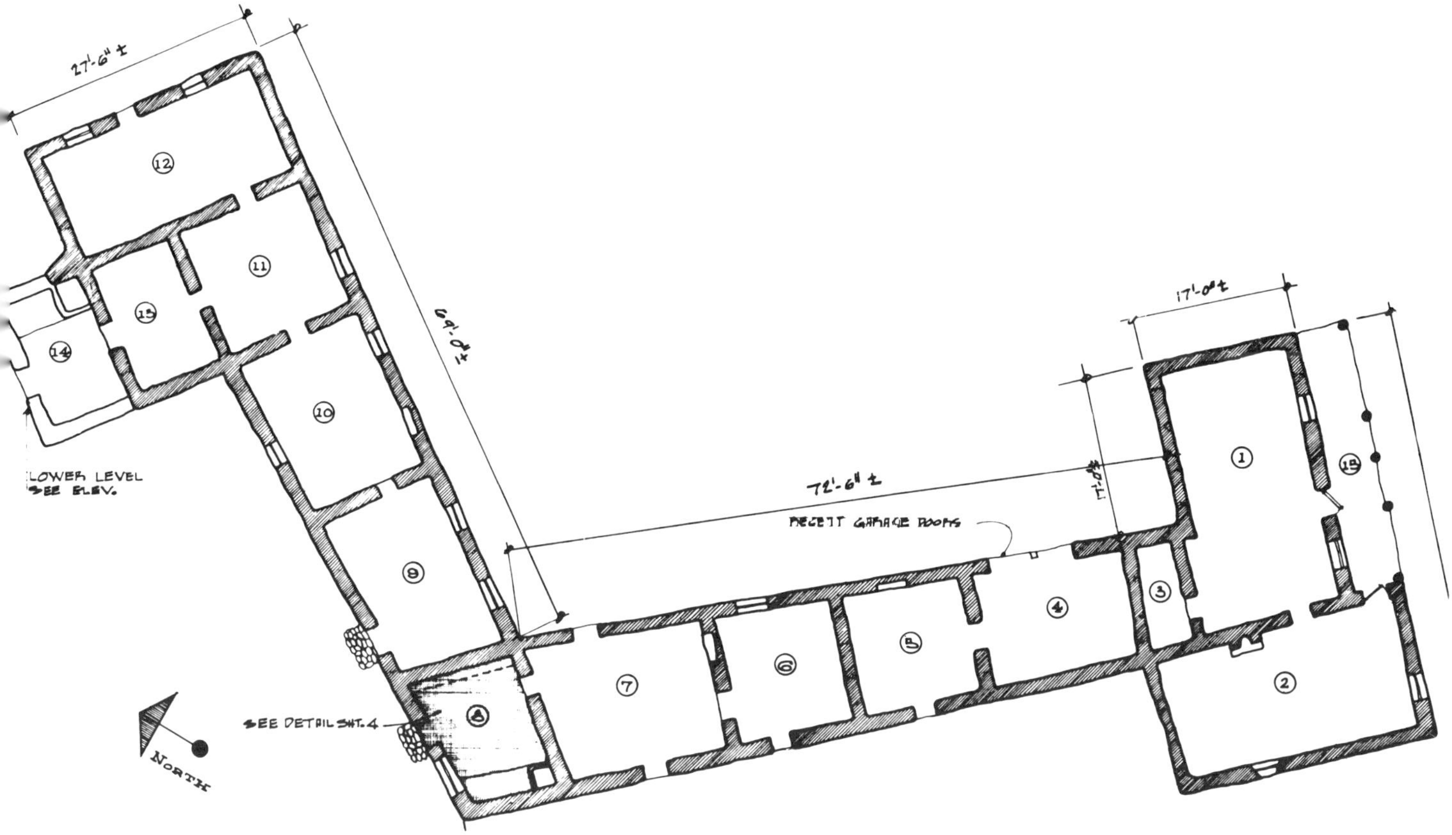

Figure 57. Strung-out arrangement of rooms is typical of New Mexico. Room 8 contains the noteworthy fireplace.

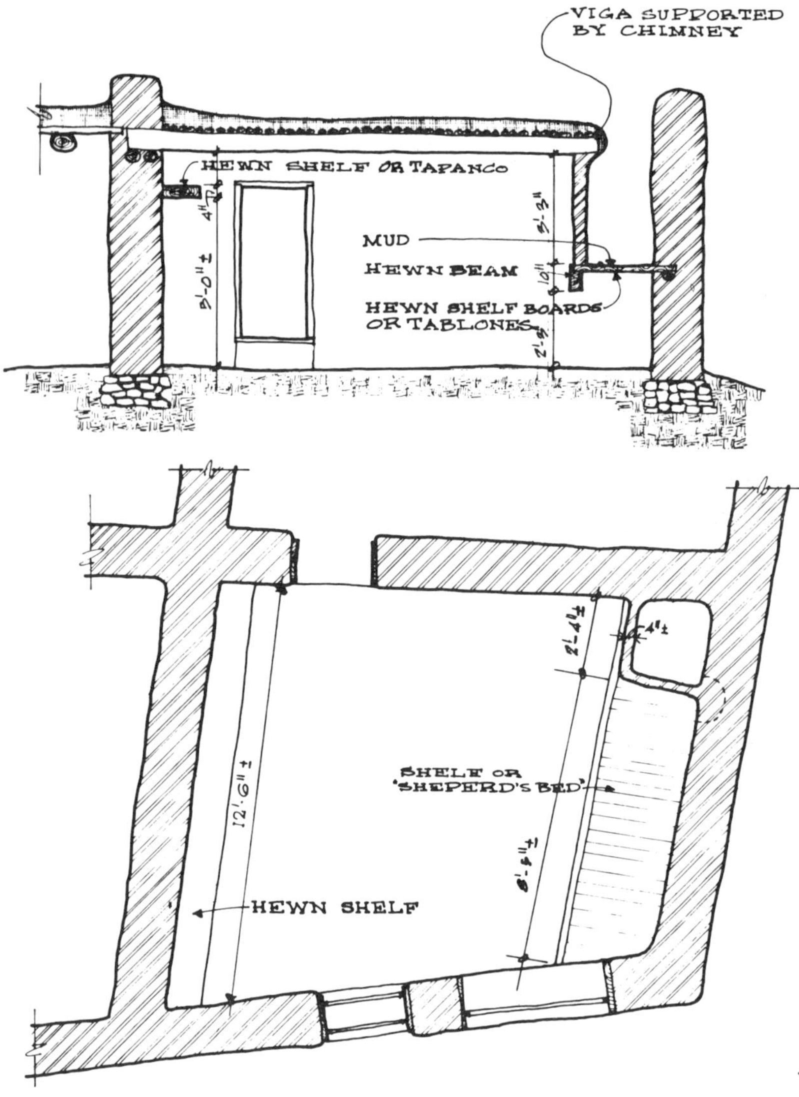

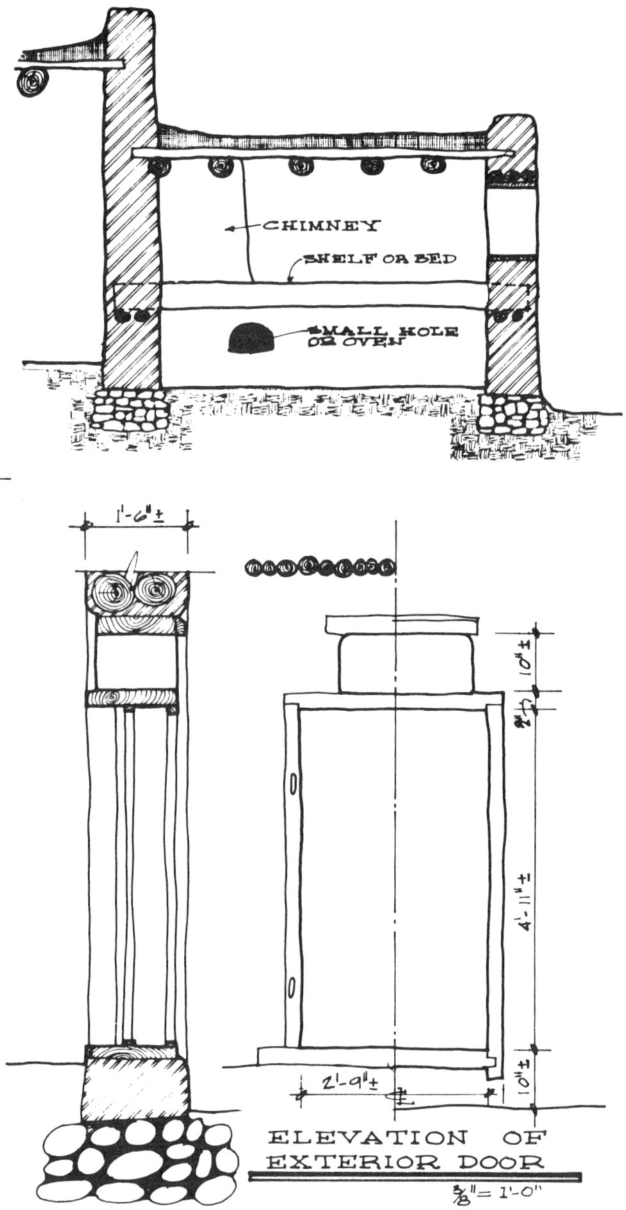

Figure 58. Plan and section of Room 8 and its fireplace.

Figure 59. Another view of the fireplace.

Figure 60. Fireplace sketch by Jean Lee Booth.

VII. The Upper Morada

Arroyo Hondo, New Mexico

Meeting houses, or *moradas,* built by Penitente confraternities were once a common sight in New Mexico villages. At some distance from the villages, they were usually built adjacent to the graveyard. The members of the confraternity convened at their *morada* for Holy Week vigils and religious observances. Shrouded in secrecy and at times banned by the Roman Catholic hierarchy in New Mexico, these religious rites continued for several days and included acts of penitence, sometimes including flagellation. The brothers (*hermanos*) would keep vigil at the *morada;* the women would bring them food.

Morada architecture is by no means uniform. Each chapter constructed its meeting house in accordance with site and such building materials, local resources, and technology as it commanded.

In the early days, all *moradas* probably had flat, earthen roofs, but as corrugated iron and sawn timber became available, roofs of this sort were often added—as in the case of residences. Today most surviving *moradas* have ridge roofs, though a few of the earlier type, such as the Upper Morada, have survived.

The *morada* contains a minimum of two rooms. One room, equipped with an altar set off by a railing, serves as a chapel; the second, as store room and meeting room, where the *hermanos* gathered about a fireplace for meals and consultation when not engaged in religious observances. If the *morada* had additional rooms, they were used for storage of food, equipment, and records and as an entranceway. A fireplace would be situated here also, but never in the chapel.

Windows are few in number because of the expense of frames and glass; and they were placed high in the wall for purposes of privacy. Early floors were of packed earth, but in later periods, sawn lumber was used.

Arroyo Hondo had two Penitente *moradas,* one southwest of the present Highway 3 below the center of the village; the other, known locally as the Upper Morada, on a hill to the east. Two deeds in the Taos County Courthouse records (Book A-27, pages 607-608, filed 24 March 1925) indicate the probable construction dates of the Upper Morada.

On April 17, 1852, when the *alcalde* of Arroyo Hondo, Bentura Romero, sold the site of the upper Morada to Faustin Medina and Mateo Romero, no mention was made of existing buildings. On January 2, 1856, the property was resold by Mateo Romero to Francisco Quintana and Vicente Ferrér Ábila. This time a building of three rooms (*piesesitas*) is mentioned specifically. In these transactions no reference is made of the *cofradia* (confraternity), but in New Mexico title to property used by the Penitentes is usually held in the names of the principal *hermanos.*

That this Upper Morada was built over an earlier Indian site is indicated by potsherds (Taos Black and White, Circa 1050-1150) in the subsoil, which can still be found. Also, a few feet to the southwest of the *morada,* the rectangular terraced shape of the Indian edifice is distinguishable. A large sunken area in the middle of the raised level of these ruins indicates the location where the adobe bricks for the *morada* were most probably made.

This *morada* has been used as long as the oldest inhabitants of the area can remember. The *cofradia* was active through the early 1940's, at which time the group's oldest members began to be too aged to carry on whereas the younger generation seemed to be uninterested. Another deterrent was the fact that the Penitente movement had been under ban by the Roman Catholic Church for their excessive and fanatical practices. In 1947 they were taken back into the Church on the condition that they ceased these practices, but this did not revive the Arroyo Hondo chapter.

In the late summer of 1961, the property was sold to Mr. Larry Frank of Taos, who remodeled the old edifice for a summer residence. The accompanying drawings and photographs were made before the remodeling. In 1962, Mr. Frank acquired doors and windows from several old houses to use in his additions to the *morada*. Among other sources, he obtained material from the Leandro Martínez house (Chapter IV) and the Casita Martínez (Chapter XI).

At least one earlier remodeling of the *morada* is evidenced by the commercially sawed roof boards of Room 3, which bear a rough penciled, obscure inscription: "Yo apuerte Los Hermanos que es varez— Bi- bo--- ans. 1938." *Vigas* in other rooms bear penciled dates of 1909 and 1911. The adobe wall between Rooms 3 and 4 is also a post-construction addition, a fact attested by the manner in which a *viga* supporting the roof has been incorporated into the later wall. The addition may explain why only three rooms, rather than the present four, were mentioned in the deed of 1856.

Architecturally, the interesting thing about the *morada* is its compact, low-lying massiveness. (Figures 61 and 63). The adobe walls are slightly battered and near the top run inward markedly in soft, rounded, beautiful contours. The masonry surface of the walls is warm-colored and eroded like the hill top on which the *morada* stands. There is truly an organic quality about the building. Its massiveness is all the more emphatic because of the few openings—one door and four very small windows.

Two interior corner fireplaces are of note, particularly the large *fogón de campana* in Room 2, the community room (Figure 74). The accepted shape for large fireplaces in the past, this type has all but disappeared today. The two small but not quite symmetrical shelves on either side of the opening were perhaps used to keep food warm. Their rounded edges attest adobe construction, the material also used for the fireplace hood.

The fireplace in Room 4 is the more usual New Mexico design; quarter-round in plan and featuring a tight, parabolic arched opening, a raised hearth, and a small rectangular flue projecting from the wall. The whole fireplace is whitewashed so that it appears beautifully plastic and modeled even when seen in the subdued light of the interior (Figure 72 and 73).

One final significant feature is the interior door to the chapel, Room 1 (Figures 68 and 69). A pintle door, in New Mexican parlance a *zambullo,* it hinges on wooden pegs fixed into the threshhold and lintel (Figure 67). The latch is wooden also. This type of door was common in early New Mexico when metal hardware was scarce. The hand-adzed door panels, made from sixteen-inch boards, are beveled on both sides and painted with earth-pigments in a crude cross design.

The Upper Morada is important in regional architectural history. Despite its relatively late date of construction, it may well illustrate the type of structure erected in New Mexico during the 1600's and 1700's. Such strong, cohesive massing, the paucity of openings, and simplicity of interior fittings have seldom been retained in the often remodeled residences.

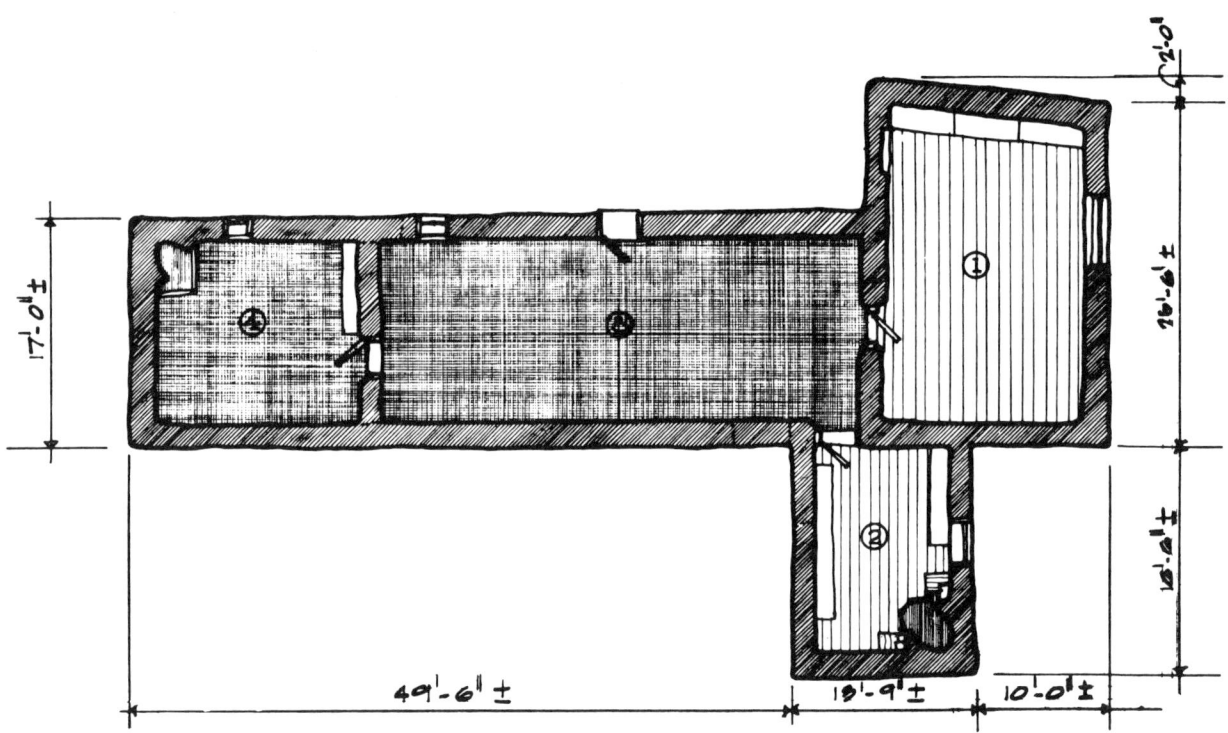

Figure 61. View from southeast. The morada was built sometime between 1852 and 1856.

Figure 62. Plan. Room 1 was the chapel; the Penitente hermanos held their vigils in Room 2.

Figure 63. View from southwest. Windowless walls emphasize the compact, structural quality which would also be characteristic of early New Mexico houses.

Figure 64. Sketch of entrance by Jean Lee Booth.

Figure 65. Entrance facade.

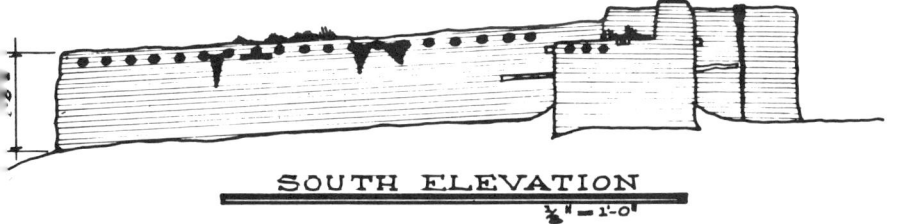

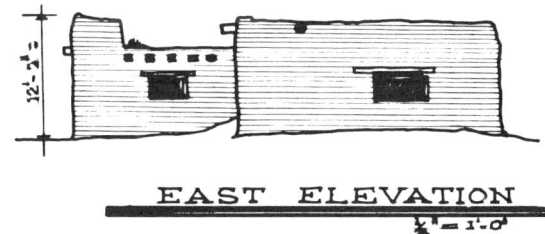

Figure 66. Elevations. In the entire edifice there was but one door and four small windows.

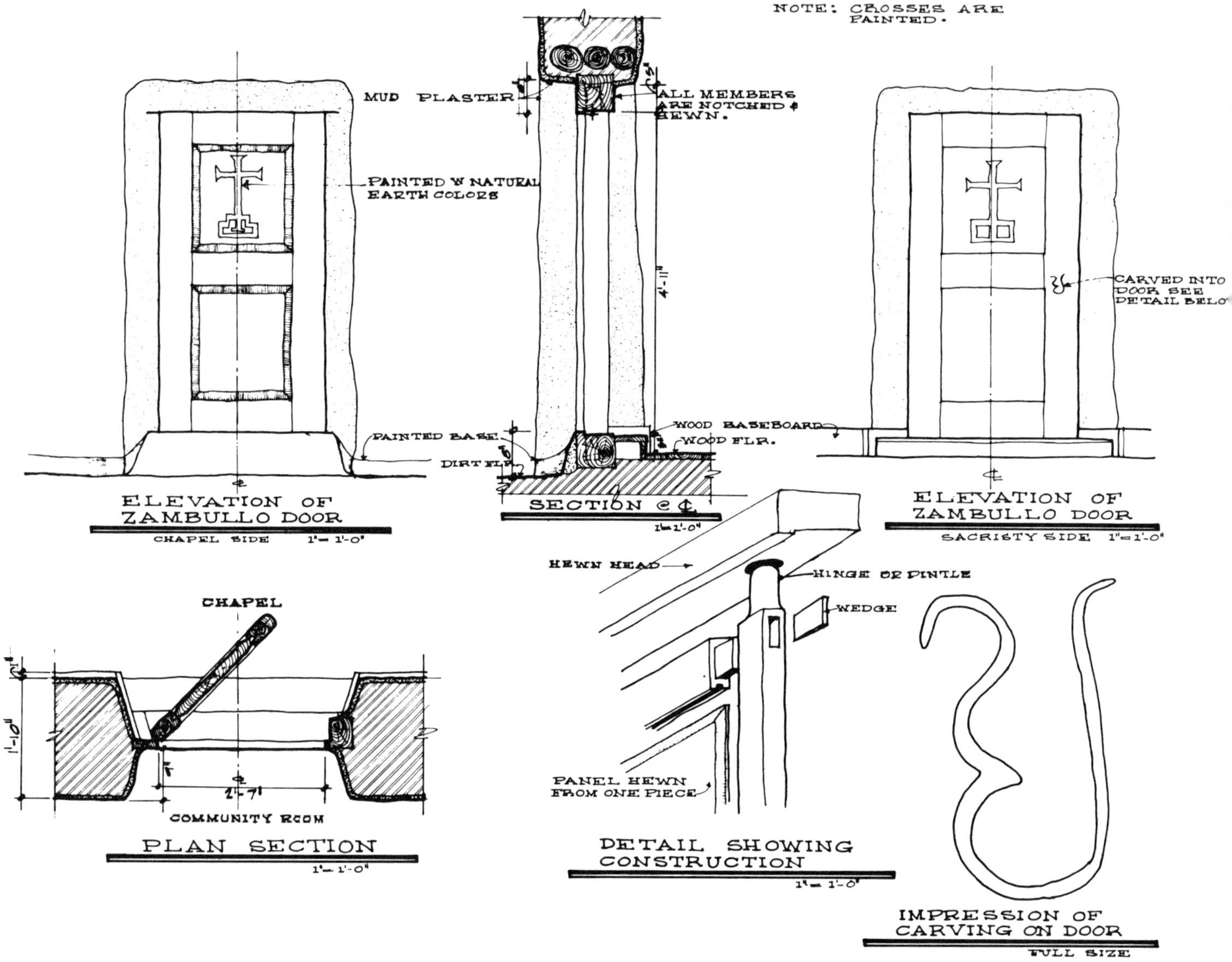

Figure 67. The chapel door hinges on wooden pintles set into the sill and lintel.

Figure 68. Chapel door from outside.

Figure 69. Chapel door from inside. Photograph HABS, by Jack Boucher.

Figure 70. Split cedar latias (cedros) and hand adzed beams (vigas) of the Meeting Room ceiling.

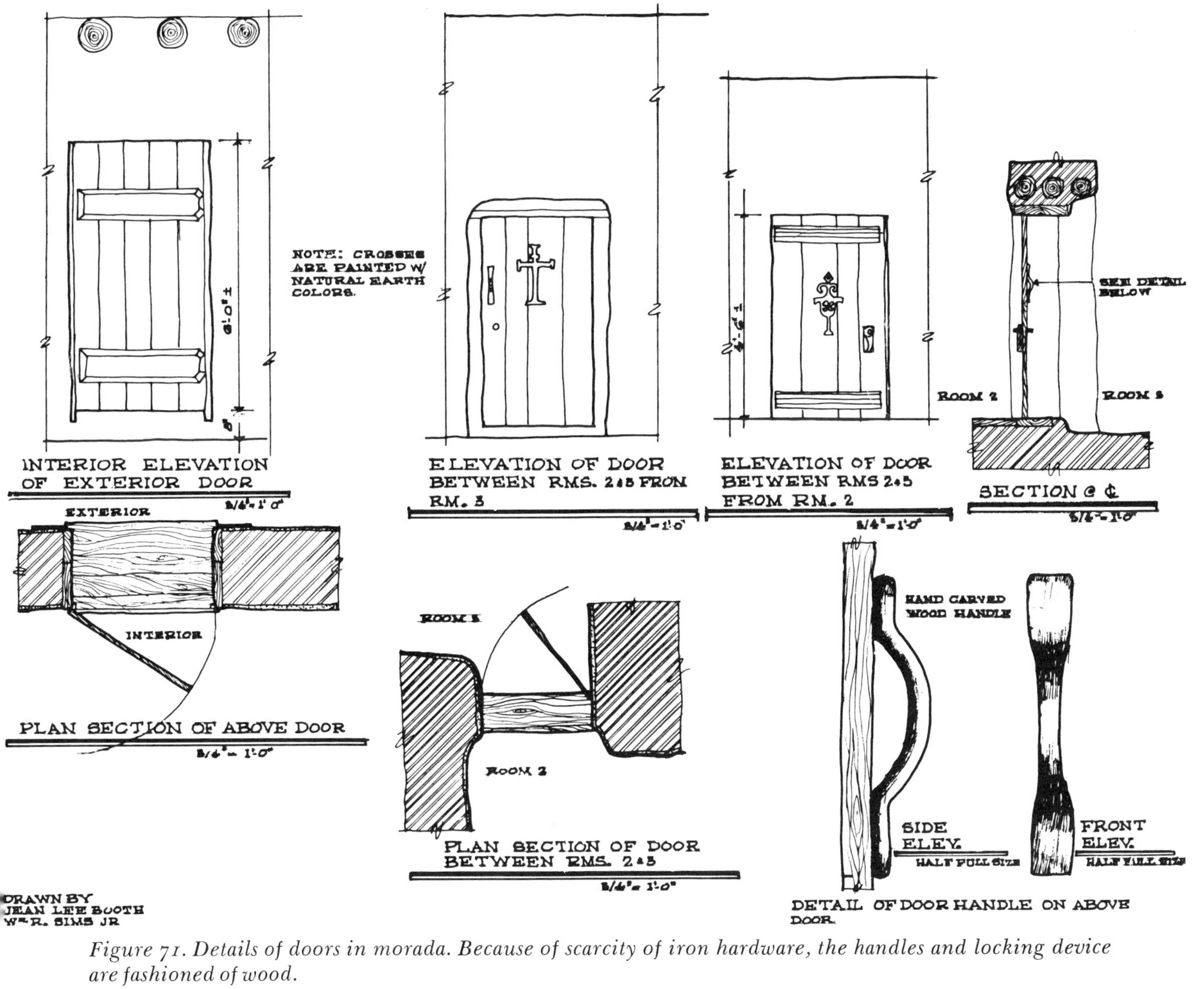

Figure 71. Details of doors in morada. Because of scarcity of iron hardware, the handles and locking device are fashioned of wood.

Figure 72. Corner fireplace of Room 4 is typical of early 19th century New Mexico. Photograph HABS, Jack Boucher.

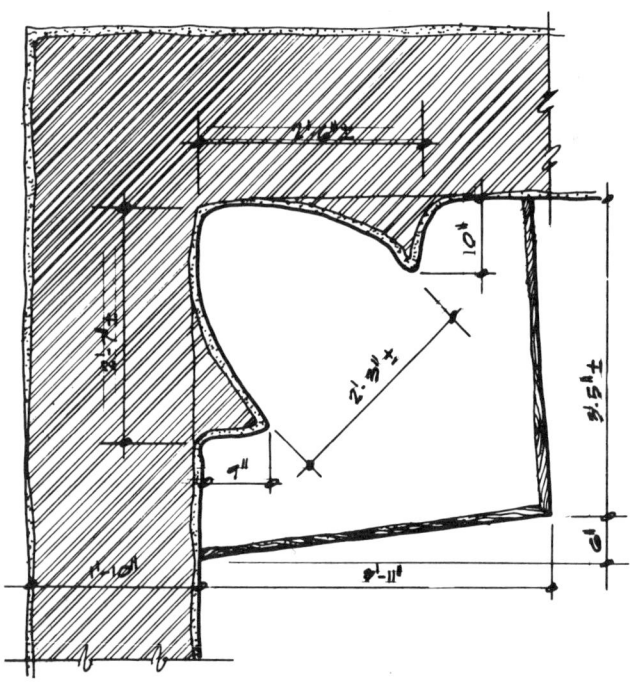

Figure 73. Plan of corner fireplace in Room 4.

Figure 74. Fogón de campana, the large bell-shaped fireplace in the Meeting Room. Photograph HABS, by Jack Boucher.

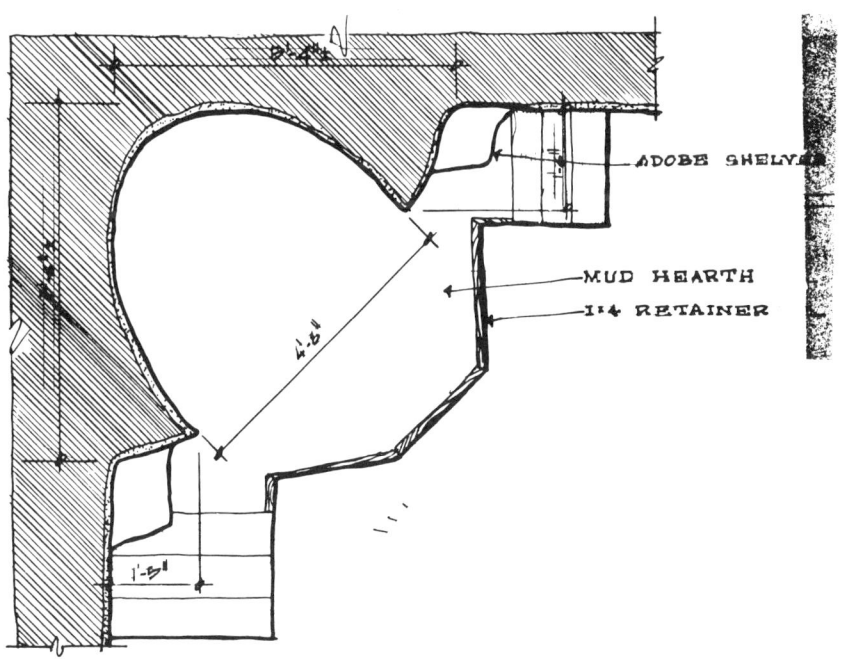

Figure 75. Plan of fogón de campana in Meeting Room.

VIII. Jose de Cruz House

Trampas, New Mexico

Situated in a lonely spot on the south edge of Trampas Valley, this five-room house, which is unoccupied and in ruins, is now the property of Mr. Max Cruz. Although unsure of the exact dates in his family history, Mr. Cruz thinks that his grandfather was born in the house. Because the grandfather, José de Cruz, died in 1922, at the age of sixty-seven, parts of the house would at least date before 1855.

It is unlikely that a house would have been built in such an isolated location before 1853, the year of Fort Burgwin's establishment for control of the Indians. The Territorial trim in all the rooms certainly dates later than the 1850's, but the glass windows and trim could have been added when either of the two later additions were made. Rooms 3 and 5 were apparently built at different times.

Room 1 is twenty-seven feet, six inches in length and retains two fireplaces in diagonal corners (Figure 79). So long a room would certainly require the heat of two fireplaces, for Trampas lies at 7500 feet altitude. Use of the building as a barn since the early 1920's in part accounts for the retention of the fireplaces, which have been replaced by iron stoves in other houses. There are, in addition, two other attractive corner fireplaces, in Rooms 2 and 3.

The wood work is of considerable architectural interest. The paneled soffit of the large window in Room 1 is unusually beautiful (Figure 81). The splayed jambs of the openings in Rooms 1 and 3 are often found in houses within the Embudo watershed. Because this house has not been continuously occupied during the last forty years and has not, therefore, been subject to continuous modification and up-dating, it furnishes a very clear picture of a New Mexico farm house of about 1900.

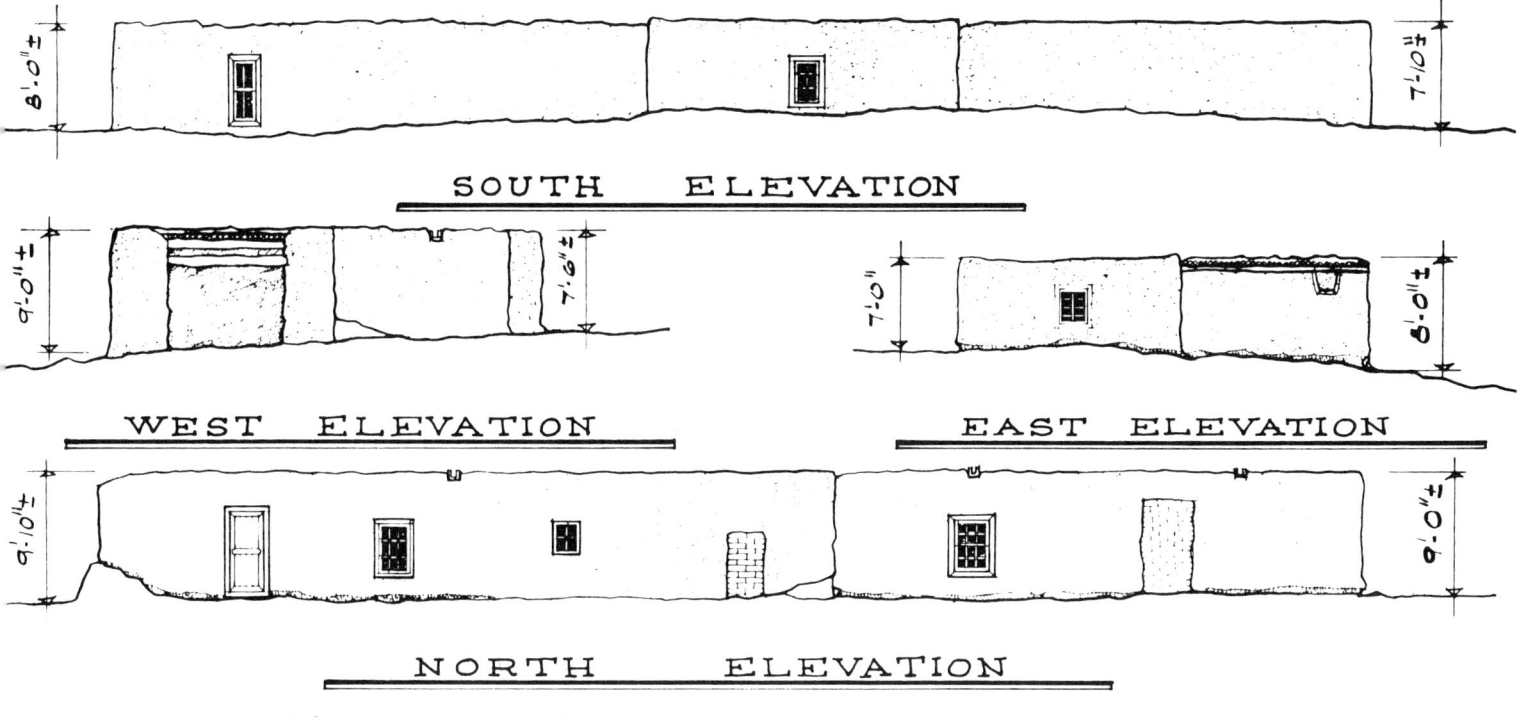

Figure 76. Uninhabited since 1910, this northern New Mexico farmhouse preserves many of its early features.

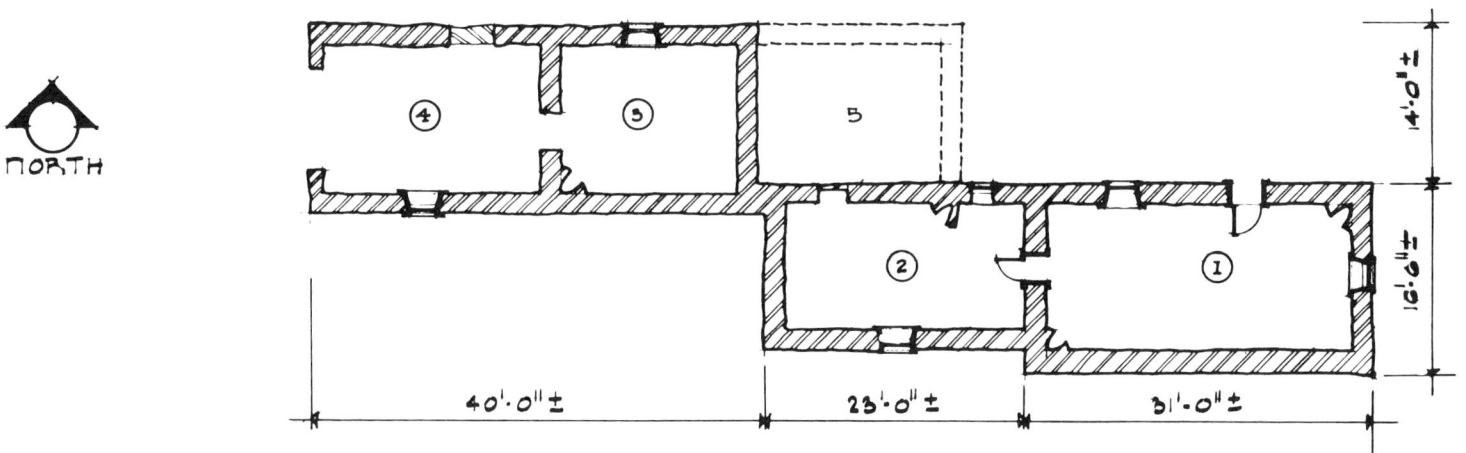

Figure 77. Plan. Heated only by fireplaces, a large room like # 1 contains two fireplaces in opposite corners.

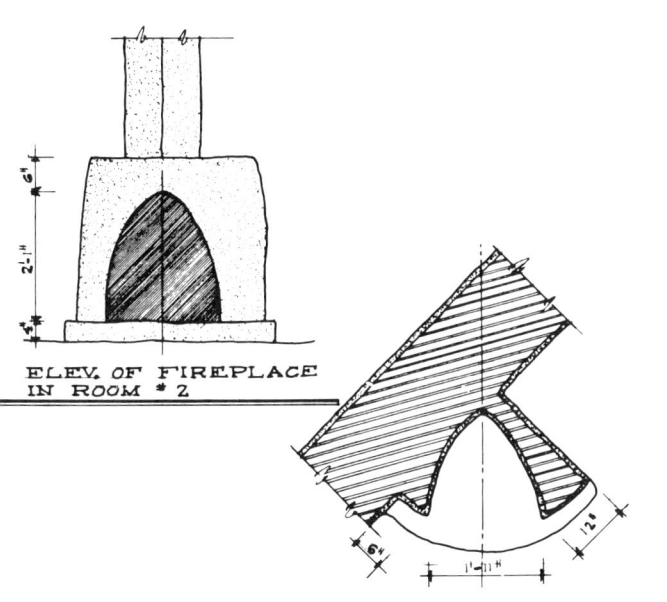

Figure 78. Fireplace in Room 2.

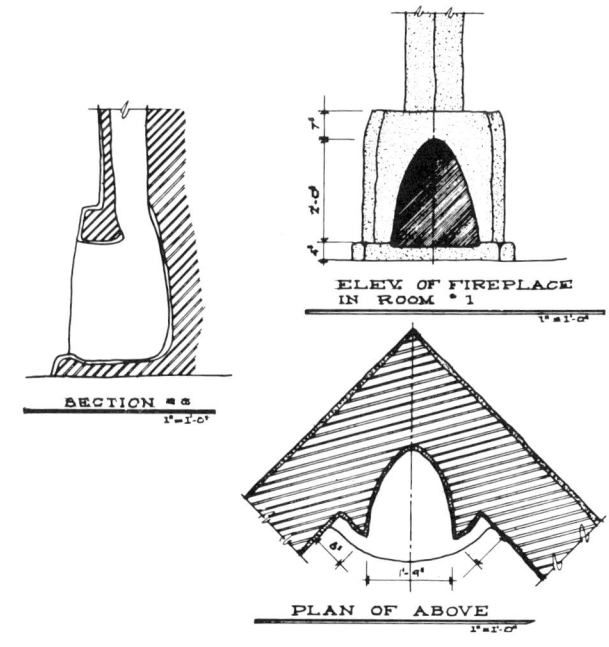

Figure 79. Details of twin fireplaces in Room 1.

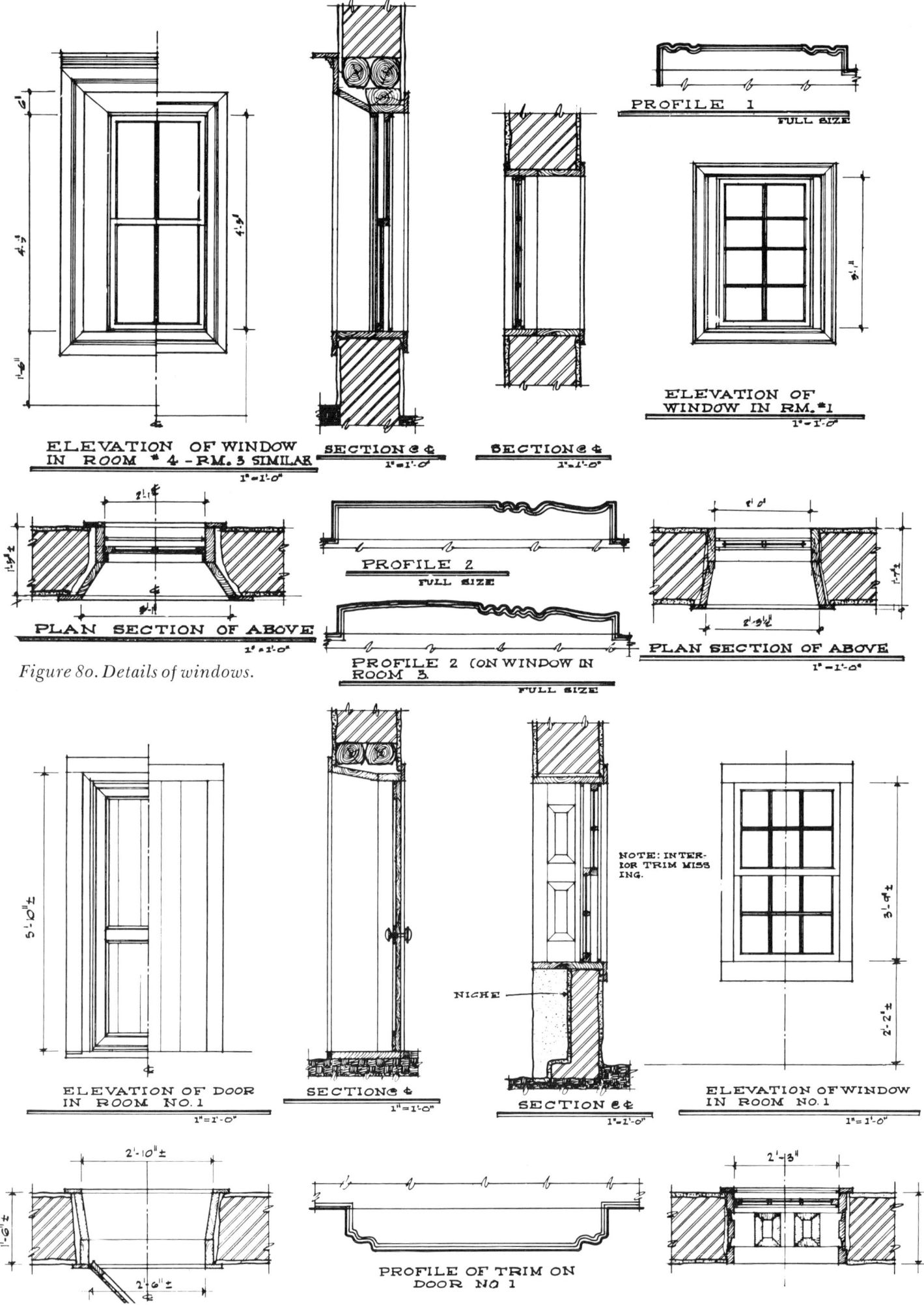

Figure 80. Details of windows.

Figure 81. Details of doors and windows.

IX. Manuel Atencio House

Trampas, New Mexico

The Manuél Atencio house stands some considerable distance from the main plaza of Trampas on the north side of the valley. Situated just above the irrigation ditch and nestled against the hill, it is the farthest west of a series of seven hill-edge houses. There is a marked kinship among these seven dwellings; they possess a unique quality which is not exactly repeated elsewhere in northern New Mexico.

Now owned by Señora Romancito Pacheco, who knows a great deal about the house's history, the oldest portion (Rooms 2, 3, 4 and 5) was built about 1820 by Manuél Atencio (Figure 84). To the original four rooms his son-in-law added three more (Rooms 6, 7, and 8), at right angles to the original axis. Room 1 was added about 1912, the work of a later owner, Pacomio Pacheco.

The original doors were very simple. The present door and window openings feature the simple pedimented lintels characteristic of Territorial architecture. The window in Room 1, built as late as 1912, demonstrates the extreme tenacity of the Greek Revival style once it reached the Territory of New Mexico (Figure 86).

The interior trim, perhaps more intricate than beautiful, exemplified the local ingenious variations on the Classical theme. According to Sra. Pacheco, this woodwork was built by Pacomio Pacheco, one of the owners. Such home-spun architectural decoration as this is paralleled in many mountain communities, where the individual styles of various artisans can often be distinguished.

Another unusual feature of the Atencio house is the large center beam which runs the length of Room 1 and which supports the remarkably long, seven-foot *latias labradas*. The usual length of *latias* is two feet.

The original fireplaces in all rooms have been replaced by iron stoves. The curious dividing wall between kitchen and dining room (Rooms 2 and 3) appears to be a later alteration. The central opening framed with 4 x 4's and the crenellated silhouette indicate a 1920-ish attempt at the picturesque.

The finest part of this house, however, is its exterior. Instead of the blunted, worn-off corners that are usual for adobe construction, the walls sweep up to form sharp corners that have an almost plowshare shape. There is a beautiful cadence in the undulation of these silhouettes, and the absence of window openings on some walls further emphasizes the rhythmic sculptural effect. The walls are plastered with a soft pink mud that retains a warmth ever lacking in cement plaster.

Three foot *canales* cast patterns of crisp shadows on the irregular walls, but the customary projecting *vigas* are notably absent here as they are elsewhere in the village of Trampas.

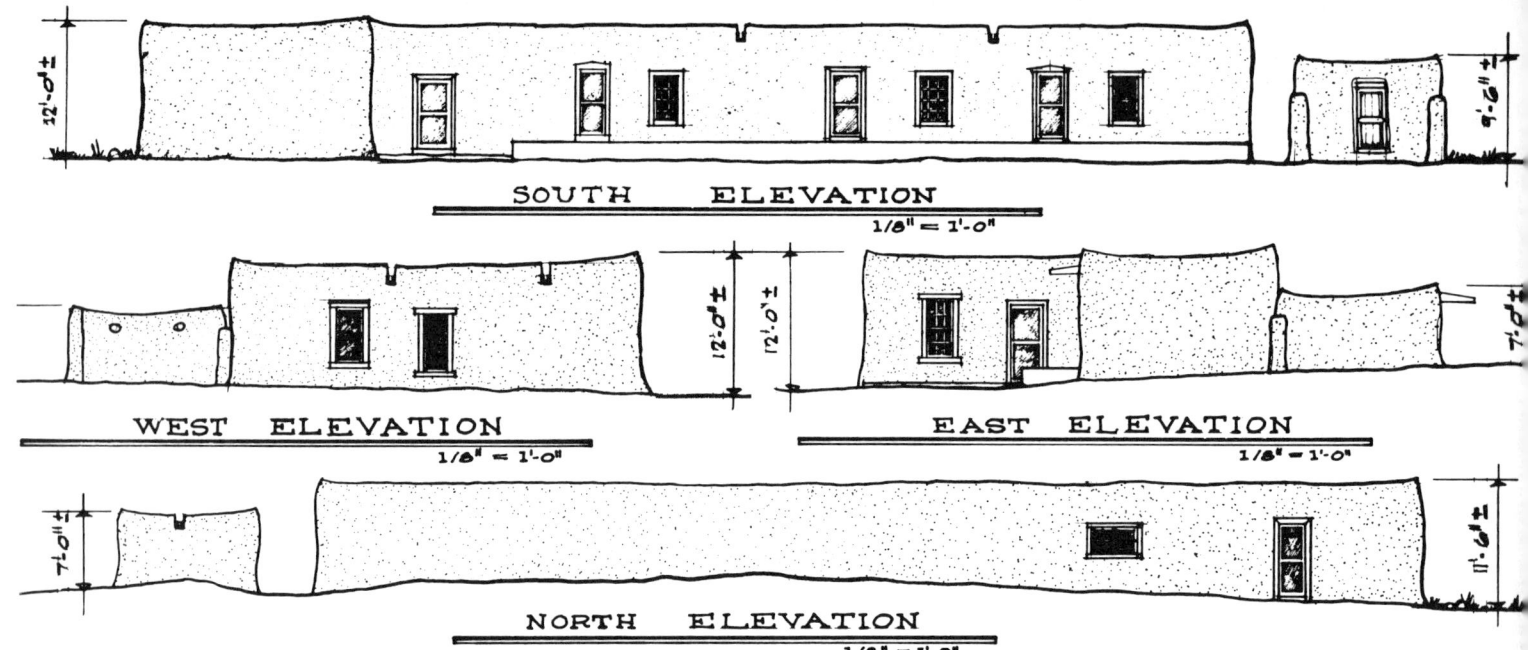

Figure 82. Elevations. Typical of buildings in this section of the Embudo watershed are the upswept corners.

Figure 83. South elevation.

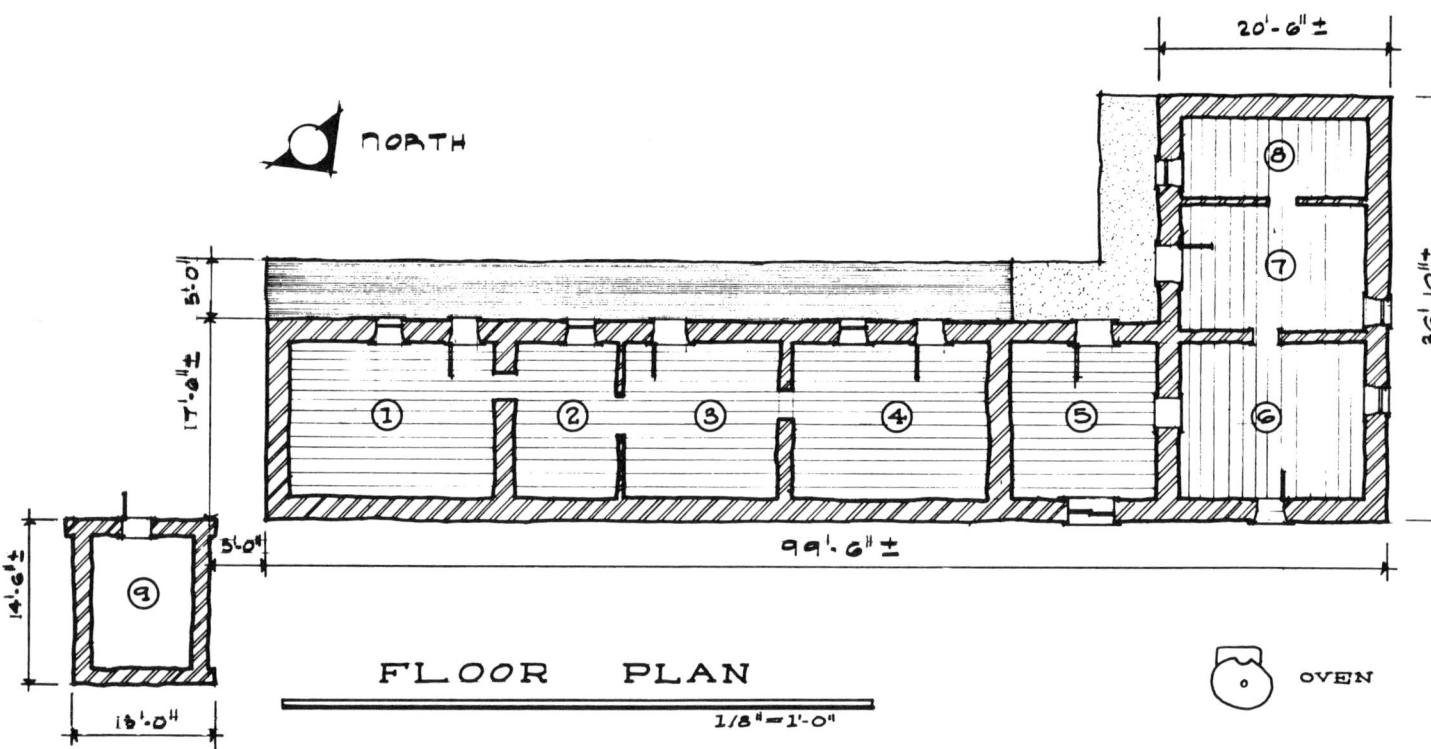

Figure 84. Plan. The string of interconnecting single rooms is typical of early New Mexico houses.

Figure 85. Up-turned corners characterize this group of Trampas valley houses.

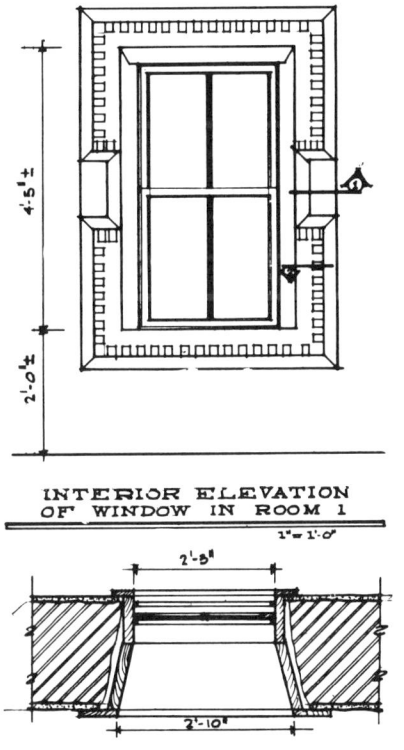

Figure 86. Interior detail of window in Room 1.

Figure 87. North elevation. Few openings were placed on the north side of the house.

X. Policarpio Romero House
Peñasco, New Mexico

The strung-out nature of the village of Peñasco indicates that any Indian threat was remote when it began to flourish. It straggles for almost a mile along the main road, and the oldest houses bear evidences of Territorial decoration. In the center of the village stands the sad remnants of the Policarpio Romero house, once the showplace of the whole Embudo Valley. Like the village, this house is strung out—evidence that its owner had little to fear from marauding Indians.

The builder, Policarpio Romero, 1828-1914, had an interesting career. Childless, he had a great interest in children and took several into his home; when the first school opened in Peñasco, he gave it quarters in his house. He was interested in all civic projects, and he had a passion for building—as what remains of his once splendid home illustrate.

The exact date of construction is unknown, but the builder's date of birth, 1828, the unfortified quality of the plan, and the Territorial decoration would indicate that most of it could hardly precede the late 1860's.

This house, however, like many other such extended houses in New Mexico, was probably not built at one time. In its most extended form the house clustered around two patios and a corral. A smaller kitchen court, called the *plazuela* (Room 24) stood at the west end of the more than 200-foot long residence. Remnants of outdoor ovens, metates, and a well are still located in this area, which was approached from the road by a double gate and *zaguán* (Room 25). A seventy-five-foot garden terrace opened off to the south and commanded a splendid view of the Rio Santa Barbara Valley. At the extreme east of the complex was the corral, surrounded by barns, chicken house, and coach house.

Señora Amelia Chacón, adopted daughter of the Romero family, whose very accurate description of the house made the reconstruction of the plan possible, remembers the garden terrace with its bare ground swept clean between the flower beds. Grass, according to her, was considered a sign of ill care and laziness. Another garden of lilac bushes grew on the north front between the entrance porch and the white picket fence which bordered the road.

Four *portales* once sheltered various parts of the house. The *portalito* (Room 6) on the *plazuela* connected with the servants' quarters (Rooms 2, 3, and 4). The *portál de camino* (Room 16) on the north faced the road and also opened into the *sala* (Room 14) through a fine Territorial type of door with side lights.

The south *portál*, 100-feet long and appropriately called the *portál largo*, opened onto the garden, in which grew roses and fruit trees. Finally, the *portál ancho* (wide porch) (Room 8) stood adjacent to the summer kitchen (Room 7). On this fifteen-foot-wide *portál*, meals were sometimes served in good weather (Figure 95). Of these four verandas, only the last is standing today.

Because most of the building is demolished, it is impossible to ascertain which of its parts was the oldest. Possibly the *Salita Oscuro*, called the "small dark hall" because it was windowless, remains unaltered from the early days of Indian danger. This, at least, is the contention of the family. *Salita* is a curious name for this room, which is fifteen by twenty-two feet and topped with a ten-foot ceiling. It is also a curious fact that no windows were later cut in the east wall when peace and order were insured, for such windows would have opened to the east on the garden and offered a fine view of the Truchas Peaks.

Each room had its name, and these names throw interesting light on the organization of this unusual family. *El Cuarto de Doña Lujana* (Room 1), a semidetached chamber off the *plazuela,* provided privacy for an aunt who was dependent on family charity. It was near the servants' quarters but not quite a part of them. Accessible to the street was Room 5, which was lent by Don Policarpio to the community school. Many large houses of the Territorial period had two kitchens: one for winter use (Room 12), the other for summer use (Room 7).

El Cuarto Afuera (Room 9) was so called because it could be approached only from an outside porch. Still standing, this room has a home-made door whose design imitates the doors with twin, round-headed lights imported into the Territory from the Mississippi Valley (Figure 94). It also has a fine "corner" fireplace built against a spur parapet projecting out from the wall—a type popular in New Mexico since the eighteenth century (Figure 98).

La Sala de Medio (Room 13) was a connecting room and perhaps served as a dining room. Room 14 was the *sala,* thirty-five or forty feet in length and surely one of the last and most ambitious additions to the house. It opened onto *portales* along both sides and into the *Cuarto de Abuelo* (Room 15) at one end. "Grandfather's room," Policarpio's own room, was conveniently adjacent to the corral and barns, but it was separated from them by a storage room (Room 17), which had a primitive privy at one end. This was the only inside "convenience" in the entire mansion.

El Cuarto de Abuela, "Grandmother's room" (Room 10), opened off the *Salita Oscuro;* it had a southern exposure and a very pleasant view. In addition to the corner fireplace, this room has a most interesting feature, a secret compartment. On first inspection, in 1959, the compartment looked like a harmless shelf set in a wall niche. In 1961, however, after treasure hunters had ransacked the place, a lower compartment was revealed. This secret compartment was masked by a false wall made of adobe and was accessible by means of the sliding wooden shelf above it (Figure 100). Despite ever present stories of hidden treasure in old mansions, this is the only hiding place thus far discovered in an eighteenth- or nineteenth-century New Mexican house.

The doors and wood trim of this house must have been extraordinary if the surviving double doors, which opens from the *Salita Oscuro* on the *Portál Ancho* (Figure 90), is typical. Limited to a few mill-sawed boards, simple hand-planed moldings, and a miter box, the carpenter-designer who made these doors managed to create an effect of great richness and inventiveness.

These doors on the abandoned house were easily glimpsed from the highway and many are the tourists who have tried to buy them. And, when the Romeros adamantly refused to sell them, several builders resorted to copying them. Fearing vandalism, Sra. Chacón removed the doors to safe keeping in 1962.

Other doors from the Romero house have been reused in various newer houses in Peñasco and Ojo Sarco. According to Sra. Chacón, the carpenter who built them was Gregorio Ortega of Truchas.

The demise of the Romero mansion has been slow and tragic. The log grist mill (Room 20), which stood below the garden level and was powered by water from the irrigation ditch, burned in 1921. Next, engineers of the State Highway Department decided that the only path for Highway 75 lay straight through the house, so in 1937 the mansion was leveled except for three rooms and the *Portál Ancho.* The remaining rooms have been empty since the late 40's, when the present owner, Sr. Juan Romero, became ill.

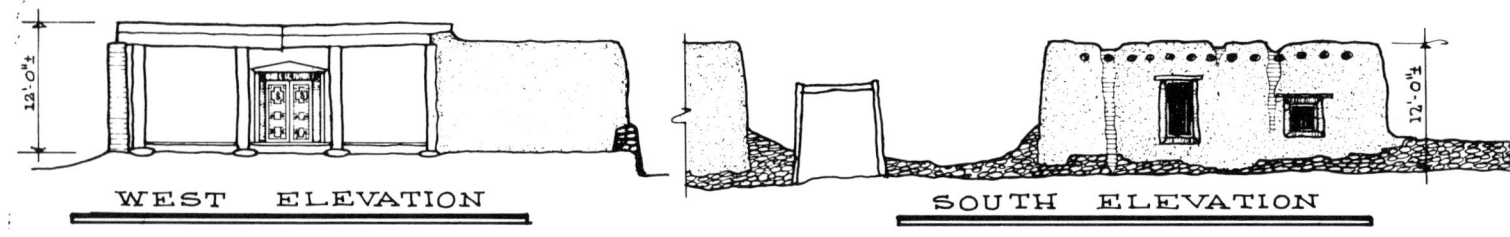

Figure 88. *Elevations of remaining portion of house.*

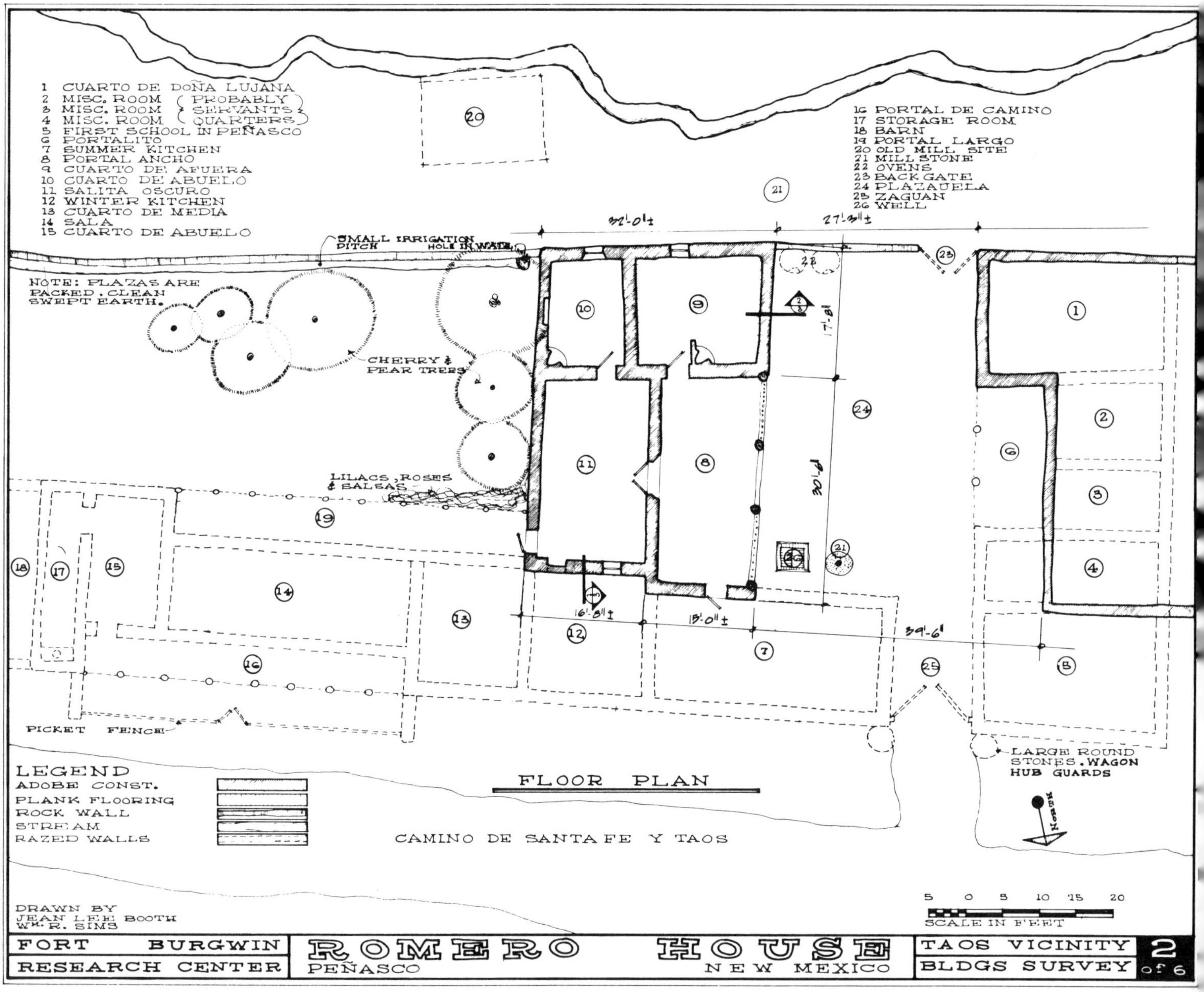

Figure 89. *Restored plan of house. Dotted lines indicate probable location of destroyed walls. The stable yard and barns are not included.*

Figure 90. Double doors of the Salita Oscura. Photograph by Gordon Ferguson.

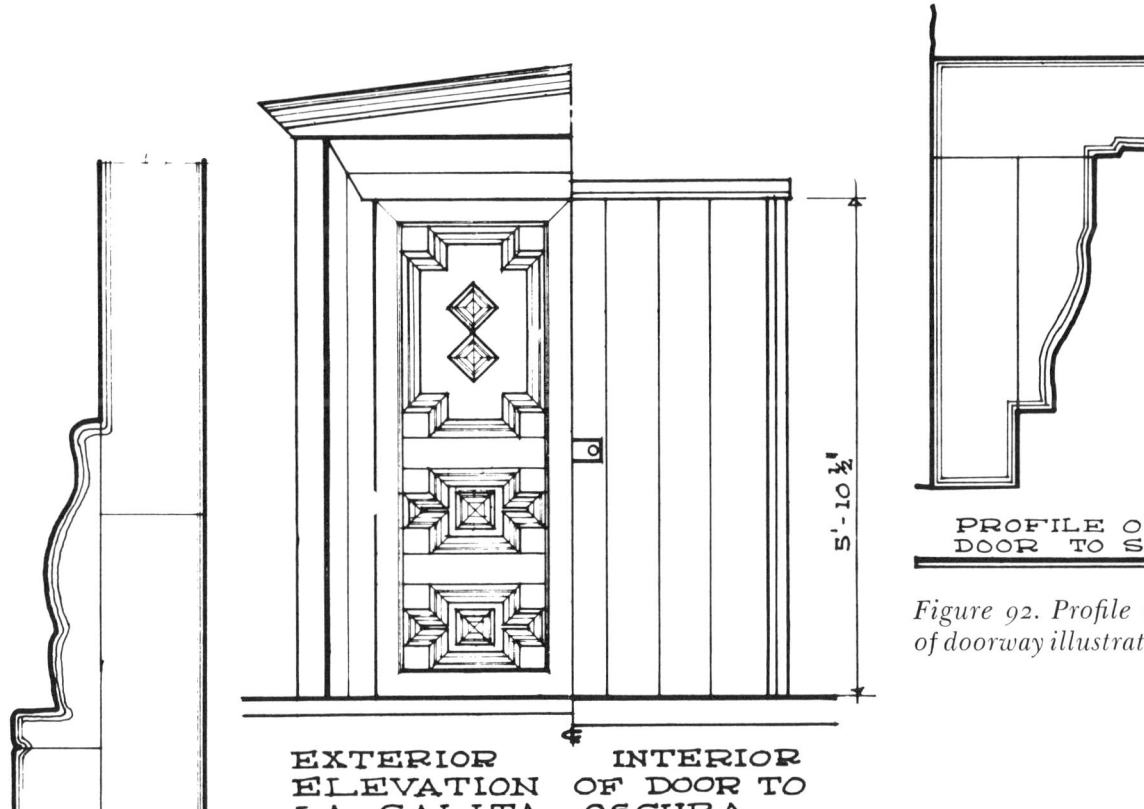

Figure 91. Details of double doors which were built by the Truchas carpenter Gregorio Ortega about 1870.

Figure 92. Profile of cornice molding of doorway illustrated in Figure 90.

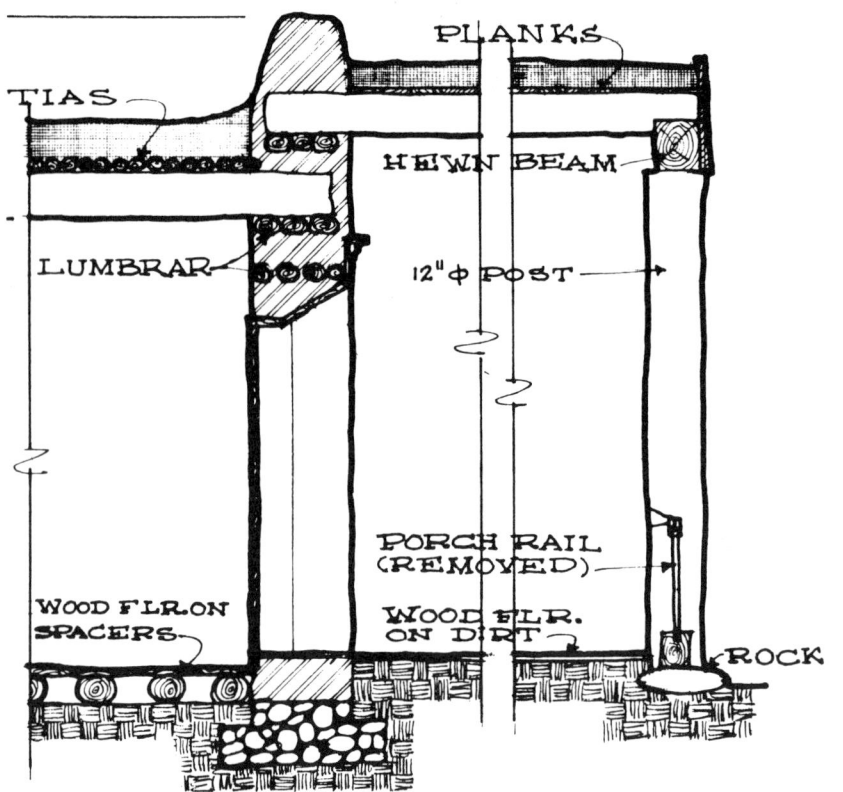

Figure 93. Section through door showing roof and floor heights in the Salita Oscura and Portál Ancho.

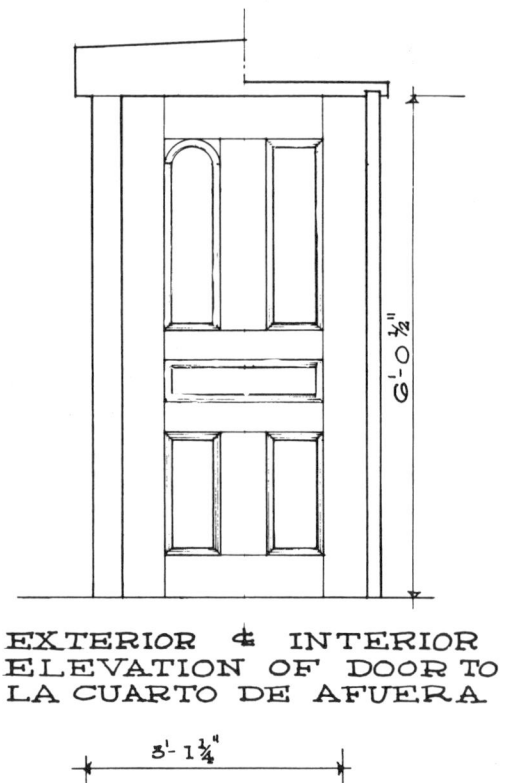

Figure 94. Details of door to Room 9.

Figure 95. Portál Ancho with remains of the well shelter. Photograph by Roy Boyd.

Figure 96. Doorway.

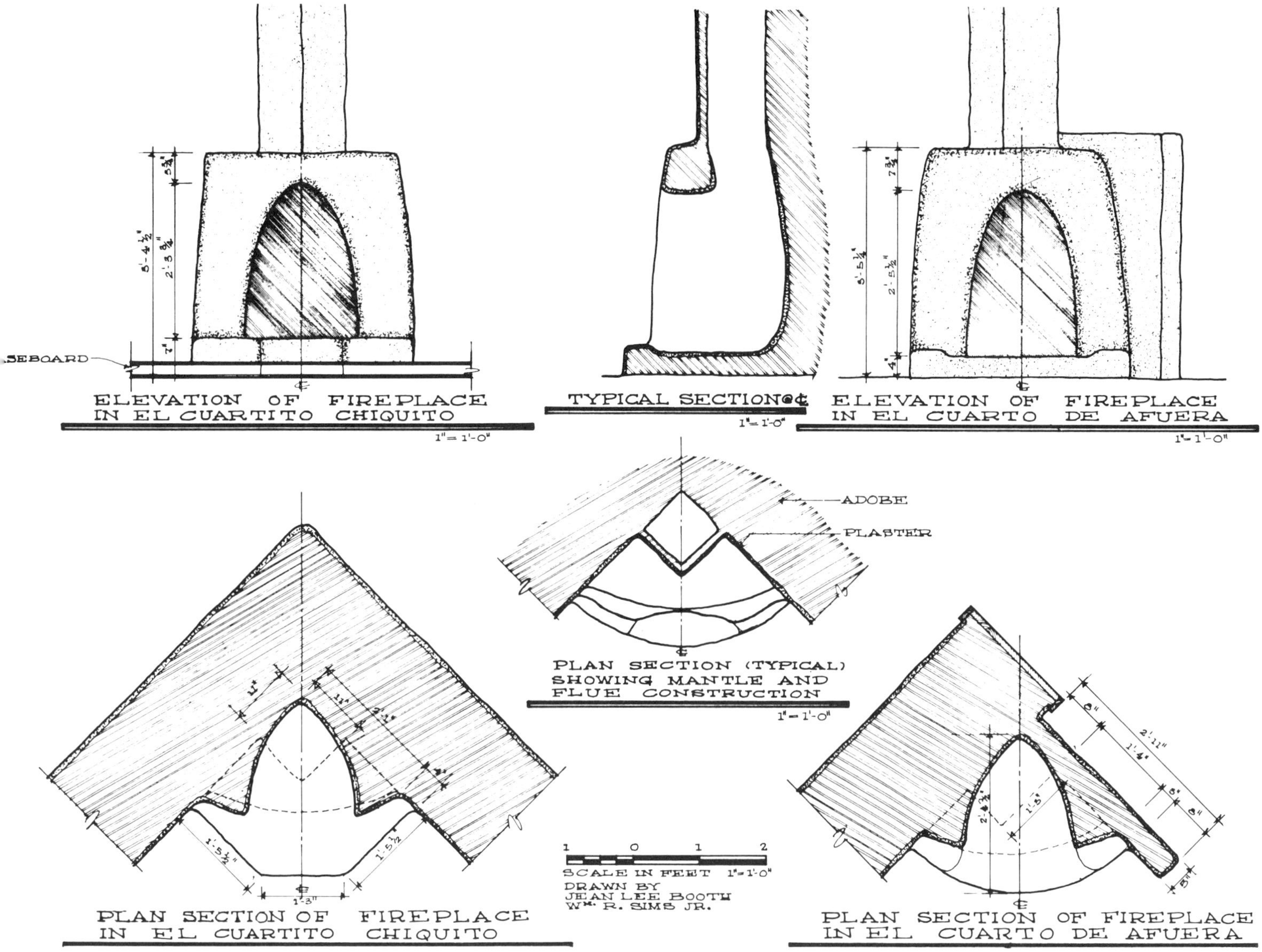

Figure 97. Details of fireplaces in Rooms 9 and 10.

Figure 98. Fireplace in Room 9. Photograph, Gordon Ferguson.

Figure 99. Corner fireplace in Room 10. Photograph, Gordon Ferguson.

Figure 100. Photodiagram of secret compartment in Room 10.

XI. The Casita Martinez
Vadito, New Mexico

The Casita Martínez, an engaging little house, originally decorated with whimsically elaborate Territorial trim, stands just west of the highway bridge over the Rio Pueblo in the village of Vadito. Although the walls and roof of the little house are still intact, the door and windows as well as their frames—the items of principal artistic interest— were removed in the summer of 1962.

According to its present owner, Sr. J. H. Martínez, this two-room house was once part of a much larger compound. The main part of the group, situated on the opposing south side of the *placita,* was demolished in 1935, when the present highway was built. Mr. Martínez, who was born in the main house, says that the whole complex was built about 1900 by Agapito Romero. Mr. Martínez also reports that Señor Romero constructed that part of the complex called the *"Casita"* for Pedro Martínez, his brother-in-law. The Martínez family of Vadito is not closely related to the family of the same name whose houses were located along the Taos River (Chapters II, III and IV).

The two room Casita opened toward the *placita,* and its rear, north wall contained no openings. The main feature of the house was its good exterior Territorial trim. The two hand-made windows were not identical in size or trim. The ceilings of both rooms are constructed of aspen *latias* and round *vigas* that have attained a beautiful patina (Figure 105). A peculiarity of this roof is the random spacing of the *vigas,* which vary from 24 to 42 inches on centers. The *latias* of the end bays are supported directly on the outside walls, where the *latia* ends can still be seen projecting slightly in front of the eroded wall surface.

In the *salita,* or little room, a "corner" fireplace stands adjacent to the entrance, yet screened from it by a *padercito,* or low parapet. The original packed earth floor has at some time been "modernized" with a linoleum covering.

During the summer of 1962, the door and window frames of the Casita were purchased by Larry Frank for use in his remodeling of the Arroyo Hondo *morada* (Chapter VII). Thus only the bare adobe walls are still in place.

Figure 101. The window at the right is probably a later addition. Photograph by Roy Boyd.

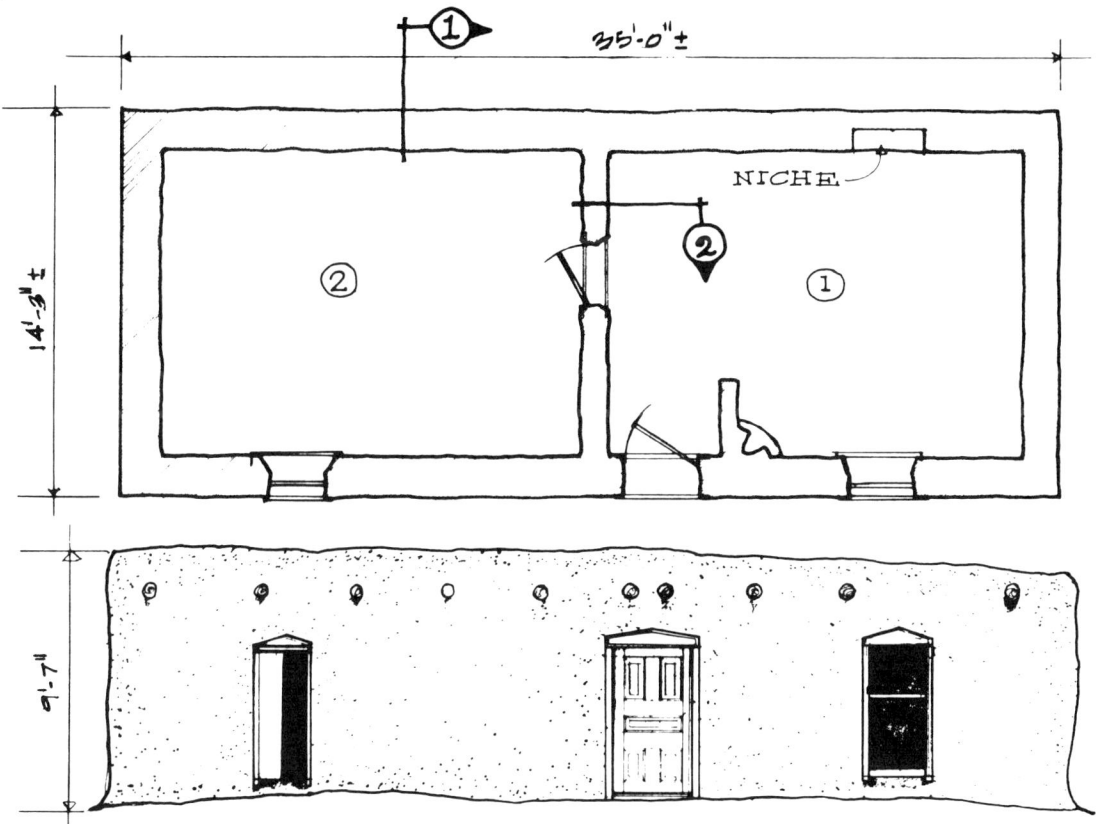

Figure 102. The placement of the padercito fireplace next to the door is a typical New Mexican feature as is the random spacing of the roof vigas.

Figure 103. Doorway frame is constructed of milled lumber. All photographs by Roy Boyd.

Figure 104. Window with characteristic pedimented lintel.

Figure 105. Typical roof construction. Latias (peeled saplings) laid on top of vigas are covered first with reels or chamisa and then with earth.

Figure 106. The "Casita" is all that remains of a large hacienda.

XII. Encarnacion Trujillo House

Talpa, New Mexico

The Encarnación Trujillo house sits snugly in a small orchard in the bottom of the Talpa Valley. Occupied and well-cared for by the widow and son of the builder, it is bounded on one side by a rock wall that borders the public road and on the other by the Rio Chiquito. This small but charming house fits perfectly into its setting. It is characterized by a steep-pitched board and batten roof and is a typical late farm house of the Taos region.

The original residence, constructed by Encarnación Trujillo about 1905, had two rooms and a traditional earth-covered roof. A few years later, when family finances permitted, the present steep-pitched roof of wood was added. The addition of the new roof created an attic, which is approached by an outside ladder. The new arrangements in no way affected the earlier earth roof, which still exists and which assists in insulating the rooms below.

The construction of this board and batten roof sometime after 1905 demonstrates that wooden roofs continued to be used in the Taos area long after corrugated iron roofing became available in New Mexico about 1880. Taos, of course, is some distance from the railroad so that a long and expensive haul was necessary. The use of sawn boards for roof and interior floors of the house attest the presence of sawmills in the Taos area.

In 1930 Felix Trujillo, a son of the original builder, added the flat-roofed addition, which is of little architectural interest. He plans to replace the now old-fashioned but beautiful wooden roof with a new flat-sloped aluminum roof.

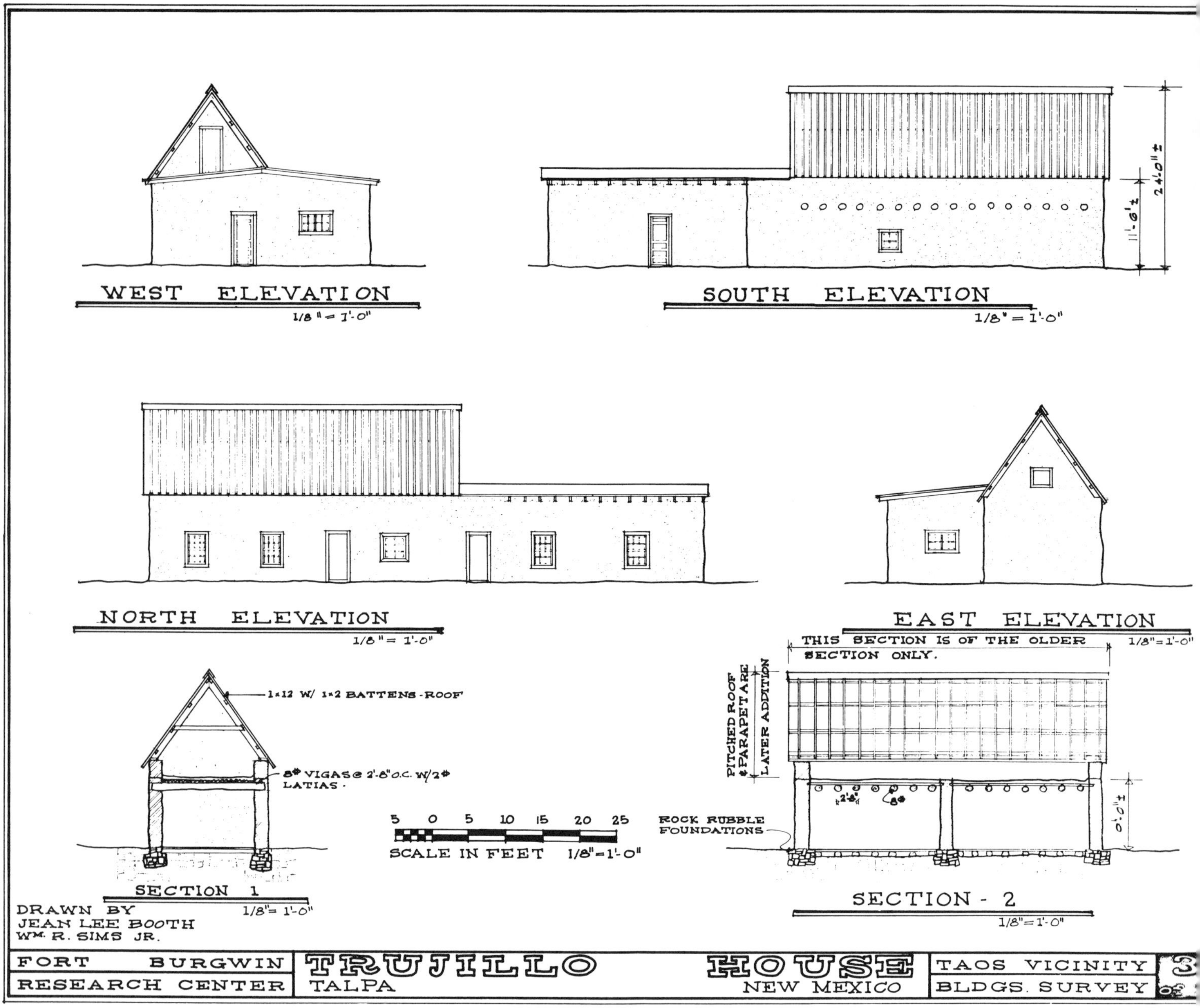

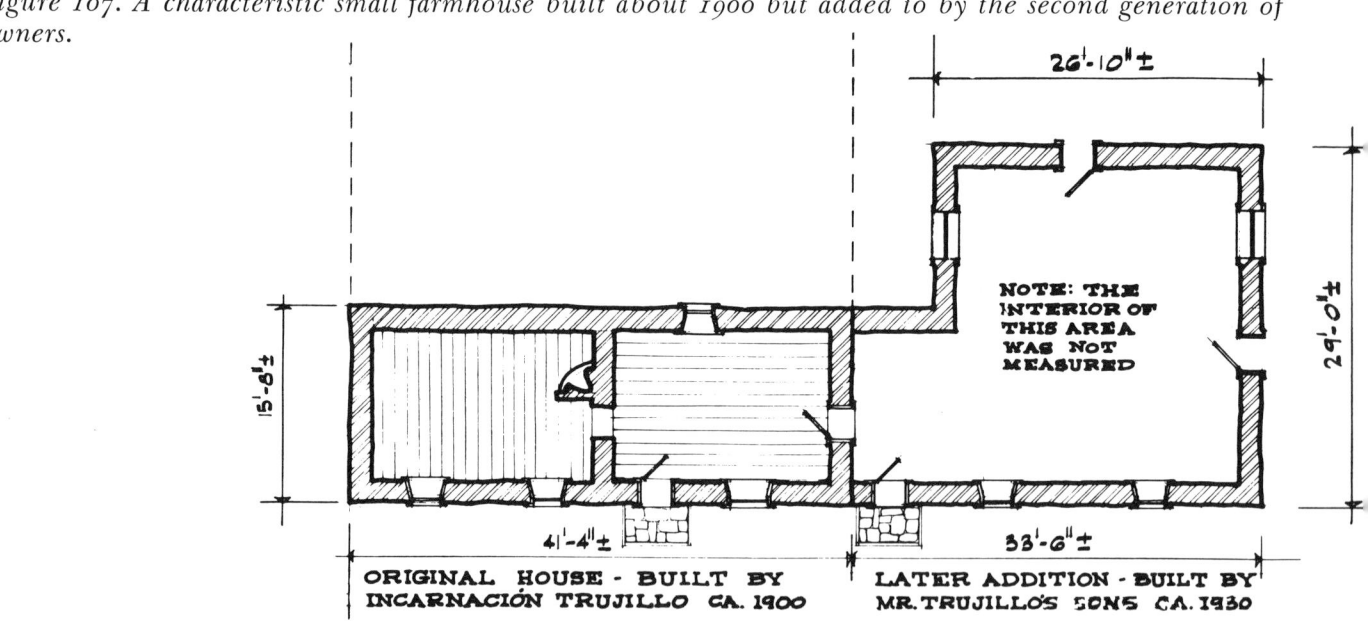

Figure 107. A characteristic small farmhouse built about 1900 but added to by the second generation of owners.

Figure 108. The steep pitched roof was later added above the flat earth roof.

Figure 109. Sketch of facade by Jean Lee Booth.

Bibliography

In the original "Bibliographical Note" to *Taos Adobes*, Bainbridge Bunting wrote, "To date no comprehensive account of the architectural history of New Mexico has appeared," and went on to explain that the available information was "fragmentary and often confined to specialized archaeological publications." Since that time, an architectural history of New Mexico has been written by Dr. Bunting himself (1976), and, largely due to his efforts and those of his students, material on New Mexico architecture has been expanded greatly. The following bibliography includes both published and unpublished work on northern New Mexico and southwestern architecture as a guide for those wishing to pursue further studies.

Boyd C. Pratt

Adams, Eleanor B., and Fray Angelico Chavez. *The Missions of New Mexico, 1776. A Description by Fray Atanasio Dominguez*. Albuquerque: University of New Mexico Press, 1956.

Ahlborn, Richard E. "The Wooden Walls of Territorial New Mexico," *New Mexico Architecture* (1967):20–23.

———. *The Penitente Moradas of Abiquiu*. Washington, D.C.: Smithsonian Institution Press, 1968.

Anonymous. "A Catalogue of New Mexico Farm Buildings," *Landscape* 1(3):31–32 (1952).

Benrimo, Dorothy, Rebecca S. James, and E. Boyd. *Camposantos: A Photographic Essay*. Fort Worth: Amon Carter Museum of Western Art, 1966.

Boyd, E. *Popular Arts of Spanish New Mexico*. Santa Fe: Museum of New Mexico Press, 1974.

Bullock, Alice. *Mountain Villages*. Santa Fe: Sunstone Press, 1973.

Bunting, Bainbridge. "Architecture of the Embudo Watershed," *New Mexico Architecture* 4(5–6):19–29 (1962).

———. "The Penitente Upper Morada, Arroyo Hondo, New Mexico" *New Mexico Architecture* 4(9–10):15–19 (1962).

———. "An Architectural Guide to Northern New Mexico," *New Mexico Architecture* 12(9–10):37–46 (1970).

———. *Of Earth and Timbers Made*. Albuquerque: University of New Mexico Press, 1974.

———. *Early Architecture of New Mexico*. Albuquerque: University of New Mexico Press, 1976.

———. *John Gaw Meem: Southwestern Architect*. A School of American Research Book. Albuquerque: University of New Mexico Press, 1983.

Bunting, Bainbridge, and John P. Conron, eds. "The Architecture of Northern New Mexico," *New Mexico Architecture* 8(9–10):9–39 (1966).

Carlson, Alvar Ward. "Long-Lots in the Rio Arriba," *Annals of the Association of American Geographers* 65:48–57 (1975).

———. *The Spanish American Homeland: Four Centuries in New Mexico's Rio Arriba*. Baltimore: Johns Hopkins University Press, 1990.

Chauvenet, Beatrice. *John Gaw Meem: Pioneer in Historic Preservation*. Santa Fe: Historic Santa Fe Foundation/Museum of New Mexico Press, 1985.

Conway, A. W. "Southwestern Colonial Farms," *Landscape* 1(1):6–9 (1951).

BIBLIOGRAPHY

———. "A Northern New Mexico House-Type," *Landscape* 1(2):20–22 (1951).

Crouch, Dora P., Daniel J. Garr, and Axel I. Mundigo. *Spanish City Planning in North America*. Cambridge: MIT Press, 1982.

de Borhegyi, Stephan F. "The Evolution of a Landscape," *Landscape* 4(1):24–30 (1954).

———. *El Santuario de Chimayo*. Santa Fe: The Spanish Colonial Arts Society, Inc., 1956 (Reprinted from *El Palacio* 60(3) [1953]).

deBuys, William. *Enchantment and Exploitation: The Life and Hard Times of a New Mexico Mountain Range*. Albuquerque: University of New Mexico Press, 1985.

———. *River of Traps: A Village Life*. Albuquerque: University of New Mexico Press, 1990.

Gritzner, Charles F. "Spanish Log Construction in New Mexico." Ph.D. dissertation, Louisiana State University, 1969.

———."Log Housing in New Mexico," *Pioneer America* 3(2):60–63 (1971).

———. "Hispano Gristmills in New Mexico," *Annals of the Association of American Geographers* 64(4): 514–24 (1974).

———. "Construction Materials in a Folk Housing Tradition: Considerations Governing Their Selection in New Mexico," *Pioneer America* 6:25–39 (1974).

Holmes, Viviana Nigro. "Architectural Woodwork of Colonial and Territorial New Mexico." Ph.D. dissertation, University of New Mexico, Albuquerque, 1979.

———. "Architectural Woodwork of Spanish Colonial New Mexico," *New Mexico Studies in the Fine Arts* 10:17–22 (1979).

Jackson, J. B. "First Comes the House," *Landscape* 9(2):26–32 (1959).

Kessell, John L. *The Missions of New Mexico Since 1776*. Cultural Properties Review Committee. Albuquerque: University of New Mexico Press, 1980.

Kubler, George. *The Rebuilding of San Miguel at Santa Fe in 1710*. Contributions of the Taylor Museum. Colorado Springs: Colorado Springs Fine Arts Center, 1939.

———. *The Religious Architecture of New Mexico in the Colonial Period and Since the American Occupation*. 1940. Reprint. Albuquerque: University of New Mexico Press, 1990.

Markovich, Nicholas C., et al., eds. *Pueblo Style and Regional Architecture*. New York: Van Nostrand Reinhold, 1990.

Reeve, Agnesa Lufkin. *From Hacienda to Bungalow: Northern New Mexico Houses, 1850–1912*. Albuquerque: University of New Mexico Press, 1988.

Sheppard, Carl. *Creator of the Santa Fe Style: Isaac Hamilton Rapp, Architect*. Albuquerque: University of New Mexico Press, 1988.

Simmons, Marc. "Settlement Patterns and Village Plans in Colonial New Mexico," *Journal of the West* 8(1):7–21 (1969).

Spears, Beverly. *American Adobes: Rural Houses of Northern New Mexico*. Albuquerque: University of New Mexico Press, 1986.

Taylor, Lonn, and Dessa Bokides. *New Mexico Furniture, 1600–1940: The Origins, Survival and Revival of Furniture Making in the Hispanic Southwest*. Santa Fe: Museum of New Mexico Press, 1987.

Torrez, Robert J. "The Jacal in the Tierra Amarilla," *El Palacio* 85(2):14–19 (1979).

Weigle, Marta, ed. *Hispanic Villages of Northern New Mexico*. Santa Fe: Lightning Tree Press, 1985.

Weigle, Marta, Claudia Larcombe, and Samuel Larcombe. *Hispanic Arts and Ethnohistory in the Southwest: New Papers Inspired by the Work of E. Boyd.* Santa Fe: Ancient City Press, 1983.

Wilson, Christopher. "The Santa Fe, New Mexico Plaza: An Architectural and Cultural History, 1610–1921." M.A. thesis, University of New Mexico, Albuquerque, 1981.

Wilson, Chris, and David Kammer. *Community and Continuity: The History, Architecture and Cultural Landscape of La Tierra Amarilla.* Santa Fe: Historic Preservation Division, 1989.

Wroth, William. *The Chapel of Our Lady of Talpa.* Colorado Springs: Taylor Museum, 1980.

Yates, Steven A., ed. *The Essential Landscape.* Albuquerque: University of New Mexico Press, 1985.